I NEVER LIKED
THOSE C-130'S ANYWAY...

Memories of Twenty Years in the U.S. Coast Guard

By Malcolm Smith
With J. Wilfred Cahill

Cover and Layout by Design Studio
Basalt, Colorado

Original Art by Priscilla Messner-Patterson
Kodiak, Alaska

National Library of Canada Cataloguing in Publication Data

Smith, Malcolm R., 1940-
    I never liked those C-130's anyway / Malcolm R. Smith,
J. Wilfred Cahill.
ISBN 1-4120-0407-1
    I. Cahill, J. Wilfred   II. Title.
VG53.S54 2003   359.9'7'0973   C2003-902953-0

TRAFFORD

This book was published *on-demand* in cooperation with Trafford Publishing.
On-demand publishing is a unique process and service of making a book available for retail sale to the public taking advantage of on-demand manufacturing and Internet marketing.
On-demand publishing includes promotions, retail sales, manufacturing, order fulfilment, accounting and collecting royalties on behalf of the author.

Suite 6E, 2333 Government St., Victoria, B.C. V8T 4P4, CANADA

Phone	250-383-6864	Toll-free 1-888-232-4444 (Canada & US)
Fax	250-383-6804	E-mail sales@trafford.com
Web site	www.trafford.com	TRAFFORD PUBLISHING IS A DIVISION OF TRAFFORD HOLDINGS LTD.
Trafford Catalogue #03-0776		www.trafford.com/robots/03-0776.html

10   9   8   7   6   5   4   3   2

This book is dedicated to the Pterodactyls.

"Truly a rare breed who are Semper Paratus"

Our deepest and most humbling thanks to our editors and proof readers - who were our wives and sweethearts.

May they never meet.

PREFACE

PREFACE

I first met Malcolm Smith in late September of 1992, fresh back from a 21-day Alaska fishing trip. One afternoon, over coffee in the September glow of our family garden, I was recounting the splendor of my trip to our family friend Kate. She told me of a friend from St. Petersburg, Florida moving to Carbondale, who had spent a lot of time in Alaska. She said she would give him my number. I agreed, always eager to pick another Alaska traveler's brain.

Several weeks and one introductory phone call later, the legendary LCDR Malcolm R. Smith, USCG (retired), sheepishly sauntered into my real estate and property management office. If such a thing is possible, to sheepishly saunter that is, Smitty can do it. And make you laugh in the doing. I liked the guy immediately but had no idea who he was or what he had done.

We talked about Alaska fishing and developed an instant bond. We went to lunch at a local eatery and bar called the Pour House. Mal bought lunch - I liked the guy even more.

During lunch, between ravenous gobbles of the best burger in the valley and draughts of microbrew beer, he disclosed his plan for moving to Carbondale and starting a property tax protest business. As he elaborated, it came to light that he needed a place to conduct such an endeavor and I offered a desk in my large office. For the next two years Smitty regaled me with stories of Alaska and his twenty years in the U.S. Coast Guard. The office rocked from laughter.

In the early spring, along the banks of the upper Roaring Fork River, at a spot that shall remain nameless and secret, we donned our fishing gear. Mal wore the brand new rig his bride had provided, waders, boots, vest, rod and reel. He was the picture of a Rocky Mountain angler, except for his boots. He drew my attention to his feet. He wore, just out of the box, brand new wading boots—both lefts.

"This reminds me of that time in Kodiak," he chortled, and then told the story. I laughed at the sight of him all day and wasn't worth my reputation as a fly fisherman. I think he skunked me that day - with two left boots.

After ten years of friendship, he told me of his long desire to write about his Coast Guard life. I pounced on the idea and immediately offered my services. He accepted without a second thought, but I wrote a few samples for him anyway. And then, one sunny February day in 2002, I was bound for the family farm above the banks of the Uncompagrahe River in southwestern Colorado. As my big F-250 pickup lumbered over McClure Pass and down through the valleys that were home to Chief Ouray and visited by 18th century Franciscan friars Escalante and Dominguez, Mal sat beside me telling his tales to a micro recorder strapped on the sun visor. It was all I could do to keep the truck on the road. I begged him to stop, more than once.

We call it the "lost truck tape" because it took 8 months to find again. We worried about its location, not for the writing of this book but for the untellable stories it contained. Its location is top secret and may never be divulged. I am sworn to secrecy in this matter. Even at this writing I shudder in horror at the penalty of instant vaporization Mal has promised to extol for any breach of this trust - do not ask me further of it.

I am mortified by the unmitigated audacity I must possess to portend that my meager skills (if any), could do this man's story justice. The very best I can hope for is that he thinks so.

J. Wilfred Cahill
Carbondale & Olathe, Colorado

INTRODUCTION

Timing can be the key to many things in life. The right place at the wrong time is occasionally correctable, the wrong place never works no matter what the time, but the right place at the right time - well that is a meshing of the cosmic gears that is uncontrollable.

Such unwitting timing will point one down the path he shall trod through life.

To this very day I reap the rewards of a whimsical Saturday afternoon in downtown San Diego with my childhood friend, Larry Williams. Neither he nor I could possibly know that a high school prank of taunting the military services' recruiters would, at least for me, commence a wacky, wonderful, exciting and rewarding career. It may have been the best mistake I ever made, and I will always be amazed at the journey from there to here.

Nor did I have an inkling that the time of my choosing the Coast Guard, would result in a career that spanned the gap between the "Old Guard" and the "New Guard." In my time, we sailed on derelicts from the "Rum Buster" days of the Guard, like the Dione and the Nike, where we slept in hammocks. We flew in single engine Sikorsky H-52's without radar in places like Kodiak. Technology and modernization began its inevitable creep in the waning years of my duty. Those of us who served then could be considered the "missing link" in Coast Guard history. It was a fun and exciting time to be a Coastie, especially so, for a young aviator.

Many of my friends, acquaintances and buddies from the Coast Guard want to be included in this book. Many others do not, nor desire any mention herein. I know it - hope I got it right!

I have made my best effort to keep the stories factual, accurate and entertaining. However, due to my advanced age and the hard life I have been required to endure in the service of my country, some gray areas in my memory begin to appear as I put these stories on tape. Therefore, when I encounter such a spot, I have added the smallest amount of likely happenstance to keep the flow.

To those of my heroes mentioned herein, who do not recall quite the same sequence or detail as I have written - well I might suggest your memory suffers from the same malady.

This book of recollections is not intended to ridicule anyone with the dubious luck to be chosen as a subject nor to slight those I have just plain forgotten. It is intended to share some of the humorous times I encountered during my twenty years with my personal heroes in the U.S. Coast Guard.

I have attempted to recount these tales in chronological order, starting with boot camp in 1957 through each duty station.

I hope you enjoy perusing the pages of this chronicle while gaining some insight about some of my dearest friends.

Malcolm

PART I

PART I

It is rare, if ever, that we are of aware of the most significant moments in our lives as they occur. It is usually upon reflection and after the passage of time that those moments take on meaning or show their true purpose. Such was the case during the summer of 1957 in San Diego, California when the great paddlewheel on the steamship that is fate, churned the turbid waters of my youth and I popped to the surface clutching the life ring of Coast Guard duty.

I had just graduated from Helix High School in La Mesa, California at the mature and seasoned age of sixteen years. I may have been the only graduate to receive a blank diploma until I successfully passed impending biology and history tests. My class ranking was 342 out of 343. At the time, grades and education were not priority issues, nor was college. All of which left me in a quandary about what came next - that wasn't on the biology test.

I had no family business to step into and no idea of what to do with my life. Hell, I was only sixteen. The U.S. Coast Guard became the answer to prayers (that I didn't know I had prayed). Boot Camp in Alameda, California was neither physically nor mentally hard, but it certainly was a culture shock to one so lacking in discipline. I joined with my childhood friend, Larry Williams, under the buddy system which guaranteed our first assignments after boot camp would be together. That was a comforting and enticing proposition for young men on their first adventure away from home. Our first assignment was to the U.S. Coast Guard's 8th District in New Orleans, specifically the USCGC Dione out of Freeport, Texas.

We had no idea what awaited us on the Dione. The buddy system had no effect on the horror of deck force duty, since my buddy was assigned to something else. I had no idea what true humility was until I scraped the deck and fittings on that ancient Cutter.

Bet Your Boot(s)

In the summer of 1957 the world was at relative peace. The tumult and upheaval of WW II was all but a distant memory to the booming American economy, the Korean War was over and no one had ever heard of Vietnam. Gunsmoke, hula hoops, horror movies, Elvis and rock & roll were all the rage. And I was seventeen years old.

One hot San Diego Saturday afternoon in July, after graduation from high school and seven days after my birthday, my life long friend Larry Williams and I, overcome by the boredom of our first summer out of high school, decided to cruise downtown. Our intent was light mischief or just general goofing around. Who knew? Maybe we could hook up with a couple of babes. Saturday afternoon in downtown San Diego was most likely the worst prospect for the latter. Hence, it came to pass that goofing around was all we had. Hell, it is all any seventeen year old guy has. It is his main skill. It is his aspiration and his avocation. At least it was mine at seventeen.

As we stood outside the store front recruiting offices for each branch of the military services, housed in the Federal Building, it was upon this hormonal urge that we acted. That's what we would do to entertain ourselves. We would mess with the recruiters. We paid each a visit in turn, Army, Navy, Marines and Coast Guard, listening politely and feigning interest - knowing full well that we had no intent of signing enlistment papers. That was the goof - the joke was on them. But the Coast Guard recruiter was the most skilled and the idea of joining on the buddy system, whereby two buddies were guaranteed their first duty assignment, sounded intriguing. It was on the way home that Larry dared me to do it. He would, if I would.

I took Larry's dare and forged the required underage permission letter from my Mom. Larry and I brought our letters to the recruiter early Monday morning as instructed to be eligible for the next class at boot camp. After signing our four-year enlistment papers, the recruiter instructed us to return on Tuesday for our bus tickets to Alameda, California. He also made it very clear that we would need a minimum of $40 to purchase the essentials of our enlistment.

Our first night away from home, for either of us, found Larry and I in a cheap hotel room not far from the bus station in downtown Los Angeles. The thrill of renting our first hotel room soon dissipated into boredom. After all we were only seventeen years old and our combined attention spans could be easily be surpassed by that of a grape. We took an evening stroll flush with the prospects of men in the world, on their own, unencumbered by the leashes of boyhood, school or parents. We swaggered through the streets with the bold stride of a fool's confidence. The prince's ransom in our pockets weighed heavily with each step. That's when the black guy approached us.

Were we interested in some action, he inquired. Well sure we were, but first what exactly was action.

"Girls," he said.

"Yeah," we said.

We followed him down the street to a shabby old hotel. The lobby was suspiciously empty but the front desk was manned by another black gentleman, who appeared in authority.

"These two young gentlemens is here for the young ladies," the street guy said to the front desk clerk. A price of twenty five dollars was agreed upon and we happily remitted the cash.

"What about their valuables?" the desk clerk insisted. "We can't be responsible for anything they might lose up there."

"Oh yes!" said the street guy. "Better leave your wallets with the front desk. You can pick them up on the way out and that way the girls won't be tempted," he explained. We bought it like the idiots we were and followed the guy up two flights. He led us down a dim hallway lined with doors and lit only by a single window at the end that led to the fire escape. In the middle of the hall at its dimmest point he opened the door to a small darkened room. He said to wait there and the girls would come along promptly. We must have looked at him with disbelief because he assured us that in here we would be out of sight as not to distress the other residents of the hotel - he didn't want us lingering in the hall waiting for hookers. We bought that too.

It took about ten seconds standing in the dark room before the light came on.

"Hey! What the Hell?" we said in unison.

We opened the door. The light shone through with confirming revelation. We were in a broom closet. Mops and brooms abound - not hookers. I peeked around the corner of the ajar door to see a big ass with legs hot-footing it down the stairs.

"Our money," I said to Larry.

We hauled ass after the guy, but he was taking the steps five or six at a time and made the lobby before we could get down to the next floor. When we passed the front desk at full tilt it was empty - closed. Blasting through the front door we found the street empty. The guy must have been a track star.

Only when we stood in the empty street, did we realized that the desk clerk was in on it. We had almost $13 between us.

The next day we finished our bus ride north to Alameda and reported to the Coast Guard training station - grateful that we at least had bus tickets to our final destination. We had that going for us. It was a Thursday. Boot camp started on the following Tuesday.

We did not have the funds required to purchase our mandatory regulation Coast Guard ditty bags after our encounter in L.A. and feeding ourselves the next day. Our $40 dollars each had turned into pocket change overnight.

This did not deter Larry or myself and we set about to obtain some funds in a variety of ways. There were about sixty guys waiting with us in the barracks for Tuesday morning induction. They would provide our grubstake.

Larry and I were stout young men and we challenged everyone in the barracks to arm wrestling competitions - for wager. We played poker with our arm wrestling profits and pitched pennies with our poker winnings until we amassed enough hard currency to pay for our ditty bags and assure us pocket money for liberty. We made no friends from those who contributed to our gain.

Tuesday morning we were formally inducted into the U.S. Coast Guard. Reality struck me like a sledgehammer blow. Probably the only thing that made those first few weeks of boot camp bearable was the filming of the movie Onion Head, starring Andy Griffith. It was filmed right on the base. In fact, both Larry and I were picked as extras for the movie.

Larry, of course, assumed his role as A.J. Squared-Away. I, on the other hand, was a mess. Larry was picked for the Honor Guard and I was assigned to the galley. Larry marched in parades and went on frequent liberty because of them and I performed K.P. duty. Even so, I thought boot camp was wonderful despite the fact that I managed to garner only one liberty. I was on my own and I loved it.

It seemed things happened to me that did not encumber anyone else. There was a reason I received only one liberty during its thirteen arduous weeks.

One night, tattoo sounded and we all jumped in our racks. When the lights went out we waited for the barracks Chief to make his rounds. As I lay on my top bunk in the dark I could feel something lumpy yet viscous beneath the covers. I jumped down from the bunk and threw back the blanket and top sheet. Between the sheets lay a dead rat that had been soaking in a solvent bucket outside the barracks door for the last week. I had a deathly fear of rats and by this time everybody knew it. I didn't find this amusing, but my bunk neighbor did and he began to chuckle at my obvious revulsion. His name was Munson. To me, his obvious joy at my distress spoke to his culpability. Incensed by this ghastly prank I stepped around my bunk to his and beat the living crap out of him as he lay there.

Just as I struck my final blow the door to the barracks flew open and the Chief started his head count. Quickly, I stepped around my bunk and jumped in Larry's bed next to him. I couldn't get back in my bunk. When the Chief shined his light on us, I was busted. It was the first of many trips to the OD's office for me. It was Munson's first trip to the infirmary. Even though I explained my understandably wrong assumption to the OD, it became my first encounter with the punishment concept of extra duty.

At regular intervals we were assigned night watch. This meant, for two hours during the night we had to make the rounds of the base and punch-in at various fire clocks. Upon completion of the tour we reported to the OD's office. Upon relief by the OD we returned to the barracks and woke the next man in line for his tour. During one such tour I arrived back at the barracks and woke the next man as usual. I slid back into bed. But I heard some commotion in the head, so I went to have a look.

There stood one of my platoon mates on the rim of a toilet bowl with a belt around his neck. The belt was looped over a ceiling pipe and the tag end he gripped tightly with both hands.

He told me to stay back, as he intended to kill himself. Dumbfounded by this scene, I did just that. I didn't think the Coast Guard was that bad, hell this guy should have lived at my house growing up. Boot camp was tough and unrelenting but certainly not bad enough to take ones own life. Before I could express those thoughts, the man jumped off the toilet rim. Clearly his grasp of the laws of physics was limited. The ceiling pipe held fast and the weight of his plummeting self tore the tag end of the belt out of his hands. He hit the floor with a thud and crumpled into a forlorn pile of arms, legs and ass.

I helped the guy to his bunk and convinced him that this would all be over soon and we would be on our way to an exciting new life in the Coast Guard. He agreed and went to sleep - belt still around his neck. I turned in. I did not turn him in.

Several weeks later, on my night watch the same guy tried to kill himself again. Clearly he hated his present situation and thought he had made the biggest mistake of his young life - joining the Coast Guard. I preferred that he would come to these conclusions on someone else's watch. But the wee hours of the night have a way deepening a young man's despondency as he lay in bed listening to the rhythmic snores and night noises of his mates enjoying the slumber of tired but satisfied recruits.

As I rounded the corner of our barracks he came boiling out the door. He streaked across the lawn in his skivvies. Boot camp was on a little island just yards from the mainland out into San Francisco Bay. He raced for the sea wall and flung himself head long into the frigid and treacherous waters of the bay. I raced after him and heard the splash of his entry into the water. I wasn't about to let this guy kill himself on my watch. Not so much because I valued his life by some measure of sanctity, but because I did not want to incur the inevitable extra duty I thought would accompany such a happenstance. As I approached the edge of the sea wall I could see him in the light reflected on the water. He was floundering.

My final stride landed on the top edge of the sea wall and I propelled myself into the bay like a broad jumper off the block - arms and legs flailed through the night air. When my feet hit the water next to his prostrate but buoyant form, I took a final deep breath expecting to be submerged in the cold bay water. Instead, I came to an abrupt stop when my feet penetrated the full extent of the water's depth - maybe two feet. I had not expected it and the lung-full I held spewed forth like a blown tire.

It was low tide. Fine sailors we were going to be. We didn't even know when the tide was low.

I helped him to his feet and we both clamored over the six foot sea wall to dry land. I wanted to put the guy back in his bunk, because I thought I would get the shaft for this. But he was too severely abraded from skidding face down across the oyster bed that carpeted the bay. I had to turn him into the OD for admittance to the infirmary.

Whether as reward for saving my fellow Coastie or allowing my concern for his well being to outweigh any perceived liability in the incident, I never knew, but my only liberty came shortly thereafter. It was a night of extreme joy, but it did not last beyond that night.

There is a parade ground on most military installations. Such grounds carry various monikers and most give some inkling as to their more brutal uses. The one at boot camp was paved and about the size of a football field. It was appropriately called "The Grinder." "The Grinder" was not only the parade ground but the punishment area as well.

One day, after some serious time on "The Grinder" making laps with my rifle held above my head at high port, I went to the coke machine to slake my powerful thirst. Cokes cost a quarter back in 1957 so I put one in and stroked the lever to eject a bottle. I pulled my coke out and another one followed. I was thirsty so I took it as well and when I did a third coke tumbled out. Thrilled by this windfall of soft drinks I yelled for the other guys to join me. Gleefully I handed coke after coke out to my platoon mates. As I doled out the bottles one of the platoon commanders walked by. I was summarily busted for tampering with the machine and back on "The Grinder" making laps at high port. I never did get to drink that coke.

By the end of boot camp I had the strongest arm and shoulder muscles of the entire class. A dubious distinction at best.

Finally the grueling thirteen weeks was over. Larry and I had graduated from boot camp, he at the top of the class and me at the bottom. I didn't care about my ranking. I had performed my first actual rescue as a Coastie and it felt good because no other graduate of that class could claim such.

Brothers on Deck

Upon graduation Larry and I reported to New Orleans via one very long Greyhound bus ride from boot camp in Alameda. We met two ladies on the bus who also happened to be in route to New Orleans and we entertained them the first few days there. For two seventeen year olds, the amalgam of bars, music, etouffeé, beignets and the ladies we met represented heaven - and ain't the Coast Guard just grand. We were making $74 per month as Seaman Apprentices and we were billeted at the Coast Guard base on Lake Ponchartrain. It was heaven - plus $74 a month.

We were temporarily assigned to the 8th Coast Guard District Headquarters at the Customs House in downtown New Orleans. Larry, of course, was made a Yeoman Scribe and I was assigned to the motor pool as the duty driver. This meant that I sat around until some one needed to be driven somewhere or something required delivery.

Right out of the gate I was assigned to drive the Chief of Staff. I drove up to Decatur St. from the ramp of the underground garage below the Customs House. I stopped and looked right before turning on to Decatur. Decatur is a one way street - traffic coming from the left. The instant I made the turn we were broad sided by the oncoming traffic. That was my last day as duty driver. In fact it was my last day at the Customs House. The following day we were shipped to our first berth aboard the USCGC Dione.

The Dione was in New Orleans for a week's stay to perform minor refit, take on fuel and most importantly allow her crew liberty. The first night on board I was assigned to gangway watch. My station was at dock end of the gangway and my duty was to escort drunk sailors back onto the ship as they returned from liberty. I had not met one single soul on board except the XO, to whom we had reported upon arrvial. The ship was docked on the Mississippi River close to the Intracoastal Waterway. Soon into my watch, maybe around 2 A.M., sailors began to return. Sure enough, they were *drunk* - creased, lubed, shit-faced, many sheets to the wind. After a few guys came aboard and saw me for the first time, I wasn't so nervous and began to actually lay hands on them to assist. Then a guy arrived who was *very drunk*. He stumbled to the end of the gangway and greeted me with the inquisitive glower that only a well-oiled seaman can muster. He did not know me from Adam and flatly refused my hand in assistance, with a curse. No sooner had he expressed himself, did he take a round house swing at me. Sober and seventeen, I deftly slipped the long, slow, ineffective swing. The inertia of his arm carried his inebriated self off the gangway and into the Mississippi River. Thus began my acquaintance with my new shipmates.

After three or four days of liberty and drinking in which Larry and I were allowed to participate, the Dione shoved off for her home port. The Dione was out of Freeport, Texas. I had never heard of Freeport, Texas, which is not too far from Galveston. There wasn't much to speak of in Freeport, in 1957. At least anything that a seventeen-year-old would consider much. The predominant inhabitants of the town were shrimpers and employees of the Dow chemical plant. And of course us Coasties. Now in Freeport you've got two extremes of smells - the Dow chemical plant and the shrimp processing plants. Neither was pleasant and both were unrelenting.

On the way to Freeport, the Dione took her normal duty course through the Gulf of Mexico. She could do all of twelve knots with a good tailwind and took some time steaming to Freeport. It was just a little faster than walking, but not much. The ship was armed with a forward 3 inch fifty gun and some depth charge racks in the event she came under attack. The depth charge racks were probably a hold over from WW II. As far as I new, rum runners did not use submarines.

Once at sea, Larry and I performed our first shipboard assignments. Due to my lack of any qualifications, I was assigned to the deck force as Seaman Apprentice. My buddy Larry, who always had clean, pressed uniforms (for which I hated him), was assigned as Yeoman Striker. Yeoman Striker is good duty. He works in the office with the XO and it's generally clean work, mostly inside. As Yeoman Striker you get to hear the news first and for the most part the duty is easy. I, on the other hand, as the newest member of the deck force, received the privilege of scraping, painting and cleaning everything on deck. Larry was always an aspiring primadonna. He always got the good-looking girls in school and at our first duty station he was squared away. I was not. He had the good duty and I didn't.

As the junior member of the deck force, or the puke (puke being the junior member(s) of any duty station), I was assigned the worst or most boring jobs on the ship and I received instruction from everybody on any given assignment. One instructor was Robert Taylor, who had been aboard for six or eight months. On our way down the river to the Gulf during that first trip, Taylor was instructing me on the finer points of navigational look out from the flying bridge. By this time I had met a few guys on the ship including the XO, a gentleman the deck crew and black gang referred to as, "Mickey Mouse." I still don't know how he acquired the moniker, but because I wanted to bond with my fellow seamen, I also referred to him the same. During that first watch, I thought how easy this duty was and decided to write my dad a letter. Hell, standing up there looking wasn't that tough and I could sneak in a letter, easy. Robert Taylor let me proceed without a word of caution.

I began to write my dad about this guy and that guy and "Oh yeah they've got an officer on board who every body calls Mickey Mouse and boy is he a do-do, etc., when suddenly Mickey himself appears out of the bridge below and wants to know what I'm doing.

"Seaman Smith what are you doing up there?" he growls.

"Oh! nothing sir - it's nothing," I responded.

"No, you're writing something Smith, you are not supposed to be writing - you are supposed to be on lookout. Watching for marine traffic and navigational hazards - let me see that."

While his castigation transpired, I desperately tried to crumple the letter in my hand and get rid of it overboard.

"Really it's nothing sir," I said flinging the wad of paper overboard.

The wind caught the damn thing and whipped it right back on deck at Mickey's feet. I was making a really good first impression on my first XO. He read and tossed it over board then immediately assigned me extra duty. Extra duty is just that, work you are assigned to do after your normal watch is over. It was the first of many extra duty watches I was to stand aboard the Dione.

The next day I was assigned lookout watch on the flying bridge, again with my good buddy Robert Taylor. I was still too stupid to be left on watch alone. It was customary for the galley crew to place a metal pitcher of hot coffee on the flying bridge for the lookouts. Hot coffee helped to keep the lookouts awake and looking. The coffee had gone cold and I told Taylor that I was going below to get the pot refilled.

"No! Just empty the pot down the garbage tube and hand it over the side. The Quarter Master will refill it for us," said Taylor.

I looked to where he was pointing at a flared tube that came up out of deck of the flying bridge and poured the half pot of cold brown liquid into it. Then I stepped to the rail of the flying bridge to hand the pitcher over the side for refill. Below stood the Captain.

He was wet to the waist. Taylor was snickering. The garbage tube was really a voice tube used to communicate between the lookouts and the bridge. The other end of the damn thing terminated right next to the Captain's ear when he sat in his chair on the bridge.

"Shit!" I thought. "Extra duty again."

It was on this ship that I met and sailed with the unforgettable Tom Brothers. Tom was indigenous American and some other indiscernible nationality from Brazos, Texas. Tom did not own a clean piece of clothing. In fact during liberty Tom would wait until all the other crew had gone ashore and rummage through their sea lockers for something to wear. As far as I could see he owned only the work clothes we all wore on deck. My first inkling of what a character Seaman Brothers was occurred one day while painting the deck.

I was painting a section of deck when Tom accidentally (or on purpose - one could never tell with Tom), strolled across the freshly painted and still wet surface.

Of course I instantly scolded him, "Hey, watch out Tom, that's wet paint!"

Tom took a couple of quick two-steps and hops onto the nearest dry and unpainted section of deck where he left bare footprints - but he had shoes on. He lifted a foot to show me the bottom and there was his bare sole covered in paint. Because bare feet are prohibited on deck, Tom had grabbed up a pair of worn out and discarded boon-dockers and cut the soles clean off them. He wore just the tops or lasts of the shoe to give the impression of being properly shod while going barefoot. Brothers allowed that he preferred to be unshod.

One day the ship's officers conducted a working inspection. Such inspections consist of simply checking on the crew while they worked. This day the deck force was chipping and painting, as usual. Tom and I had been assigned to paint around the base of the superstructure with red lead. Red lead is primer that is used as an under coat to prevent rust and is subsequently painted over with grey, white, yellow or black lead depending on the area of the ship.

The CO, with the ship's complement of officers in order of chain of command behind him, strolled towards our position as Tom and I painted. With a snicker Tom said, " Hey watch this, Mal."

Tom continued to paint until the Captain passed and when the XO walked by he slapped a two-inch riser adjacent to the superstructure bulk head with his paint brush full of red lead. That swift and silent stroke sent a line of red paint droplets right up the XO's back. Behind the XO the Warrant Officer snickered, but did not have the guts to say anything to the XO. As he passed Tom gave the brush a little pop across the two-inch riser and sent a line of red lead drops up the Warrant Officer's back - and so on through the procession of officers. Each officer in line unwilling to tattle on Tom and each getting the same treatment in turn.

During one general quarters drill Tom received his comeuppance for the red lead incident. On any ship when general quarters is sounded the crew must run full tilt to their battle stations. Specific routes for getting to your assigned battle station are mandatory. To keep a traffic jam from impeding the crew there are rules. If your battle station is forward you run along the starboard side. If your station is aft you run along the port side. I was standing with Tom next to the port side life boat when general quarters sounded and he took off at top speed towards the bow of the ship - against the traffic. The moment Tom acquired full tilt a steel compartment door swung open and he hit full force. The door rang like a gong and Tom hit the deck, out cold.

Usually during a drill of this nature someone would be assigned as casualty dummy. On this day Tom Brothers *was* the casualty dummy. We loaded him onto a stretcher and practiced with him for quite a while before he regained consciousness.

That was not the only time Tom thwacked himself into unconsciousness. During a patrol in the Bay of Campeche we had a rare opportunity for a swim call. Swim call is one of the few ways for the Captian to relieve the crew from the monotony of open sea duty. The Gulf of Campeche can be one hot son-of-a-bitch in the summer. As cold as steel will get when left outside during an winter's night, so hot it will become when exposed to the blistering rays of a tropical sun. The steel deck of a ship can become almost unbearable to walk, and below deck the radiant heat factor is stifling- hence, swim call.

During swim call, it was not only customary but mandatory to post a look out on the flying bridge armed with a WW II vintage M1 carbine, in the event sharks were attracted by flailing swimmers. Tom Brothers thought it would be a marvelous idea to climb to the flying bridge where the shark look-out was posted and dive off the rail. When he had mounted the flying bridge and as he balanced on the rail, he yelled to all the swimmers.

"Hey mates - watch this!"

As he released the compression of his knees to spring off the rail in the graceful arc of a swan dive the ship rolled into him. Of course, it was too late. Tom was committed - to the air. From the water we saw a guy trying in earnest to crawl forward through the air - a frantic effort to clear the deck. We could see a look of utter terror in his face and we thought it part of his usual act. It did not occur to us that he was actually in trouble. It would have been a comical site had Tom cleared the deck and made the water. But he didn't and it wasn't. He came full force into the flat of the deck and was knocked out cold with a concussion and dislocated shoulder. He had to be med-evaced out. Swim call was abruptly terminated.

On the Dione, anyone senior to you could assign extra duty. Tom Brothers and I were junior to everybody on the Dione. Once Tom returned to the ship, after some serious recovery time, he was up to his old shenanigans and our tours of extra duty had become increasing and frequent. In fact, it got so ridiculous that when assigned extra duty for some screwup, or spending quality time with "Ole Shep" the dog instead of working, we would often quip "I got two hours, will someone give me four?" Once too often to my taste.

During one patrol out of Freeport, Brothers was up to everything but his assigned duty and I happened to be assigned with him, when literally out of the blue came–

"Smith. Brothers," Mickey Mouse barked, "That'll be two hours each - extra duty."

"I'll see your two - will some one give me four?" quipped Tom.

"Oh shit," I thought, "Here we go."

"O.K., Mister. Four hours extra duty - your buddy here too," replied Mickey.

"I got four will anybody give me six?" challenged Brothers.

"Restricted to the dock when we return to port - both of you," intoned Mickey. "And you take the extra duty tonight - both," he added.

That is how it came to pass that Tom Brothers and I were restricted to the ship while docked in Freeport, Texas as Tom prepared to exact revenge on his nemesis, Mickey Mouse. One evening Tom and I were hauling trash to the dock side dumpster. After we dumped the load, Tom snuck over to the parking lot and I could see him doing something under the front of Mickey's car. The parking lot - hell, all the roads - hell, everything on the Gulf Coast is covered with crushed oyster shells. There ain't no gravel on the Gulf Coast. Tom was in the shell-covered lot with a border of old telephone poles as bumpers. He squatted between the old telephone pole and the front of Mickey's car. It was parked nose in against the pole. Quickly, Tom stood up and came running the hundred or so feet back to the dock.

"Hurry up Smitty," he cautioned as he scampered up the gangway.

I followed quickly. We lollygagged on deck, but out of the way. Moments later Mickey Mouse walked down the gangway, and over to the parking lot.

"Watch this," Brothers said, while nudging me into a better viewing position.

Mickey got in his brand new Buick and fired it up, slammed it into reverse and trounced the gas. Every night the Dione was in port, Mickey left for home in just this same manner - crushed oyster shells were flyin'. The car flew backwards out of the parking space and just before the point were any normal person would hit the brakes and spin the wheel, Mickey goosed the gas a little, instead of the brake. He cranked the wheel in an attempt to broady the front end around. Just at the critical moment, the car shuddered.

The steering wheel came spinning back, slapping the be-jesus out of his knuckles - "Thwackity - thwack- thwack." Like a nun with a ruler on a bad prayer day.

Mickey put it in park and got out, alternately wringing then shaking his hands. He walked to the front of the car and there lay the bumper, hooked to a chain, wrapped around the telephone pole bumper. He stormed the gang-way, crimson-faced.

The entire crew had to stand muster, until somebody 'fessed up for that one. Nobody did. The XO eventually let us stand down, after a good tirade and serious extra duty for all, except of course for Chief Patterson, who would supervise it. Except this supervisory capacity actually represented *extra duty* for the Chief. He did not like it.

It is said in naval annals (somewhere, I'm sure), that the Chief of the Boat is next to God. On the Dione, God was Chief Patterson. The Captain knew it, the XO knew it, the crew knew it and the Chief damn sure knew it. God, how that man hated me. The only person he hated more was Tom Brothers.

Shortly after the chain-jerking of Mickey Mouse and the subsequent and interminable extra duty suffered by all and to exact his revenge for the whole incident which had caused him - *The Chief of the Freakin' Boat* - so much extra duty, Chief Patterson started to assign Tom and I extra duty during lunch break. Hence, this day Tom was assigned to paint one of the masts, the tallest one at the top, of course. I was assigned painting and scraping on the deck, as usual. As we worked our way through the lunch hour, Chief Patterson began his perfunctory stroll and gloat by and over the seamen he has on extra duty. He whistled and carried the grin of a man exacting a toll. He reveled in his power as he strolled the deck, belly full of lunch.

From above, at the very mast head where the radar dish spins, I heard.

"Hey! Mal, watch this!"

I looked up to see Tom feigning a pour of paint to the deck as the Chief approached. I shook my head "NO" - the Chief kept strolling. Tom started to pour the paint - the Chief kept strolling. All taking place in slow motion. Once under the mast, Tom called out from above.

"Hey Chief, watch out!"

The Chief looked up. He was struck and covered by a falling curtain of black paint, again all in slow motion to my eye. To make matters worse, Tom let the bucket follow the paint. The empty bucket struck the Chief on the pate. Despite Tom's plea that accidents do happen, the Chief scaled the mast and had Brothers at bay in seconds. Tom kicked at him while astraddle of the radar dish, and vociferously pled his innocence. The Chief cursed him and threatened to "throw his ass off the mast head," and he would have if the XO had not ordered them both down to the deck.

To my knowledge after the incident Tom Brothers was never permitted a moment's peace to eat lunch on the Dione again. Each day while the rest of the crew ate lunch, Tom scraped or painted.

Another guy Tom liked to mess with was the apprentice cook by the name of Mol. I never knew the guy's first name - everybody just called him Mol. Mol was a social oddity. If you treated him with kid gloves he would feed you good, even sneak food to you, but you could incite him to physical violence with an innocuous, insulting joke. Tom Brothers liked to pull Mol's chain frequently.

Considering the Dione was built in 1930 and that it was not the berth any seafarer of experience would pay for passage on, and that it was, after all, a military ship, it came as no surprise the head was only one technological advance above outhouse. In the head of this old ship were stools with an open trough running under each. From the bulkhead, small partitions jutted out between each stool to afford the user some semblance of privacy. One morning while Mol was occupied with his business on the last stool in the line, before the trough and its contents exit the head to God only knew where (and thanks to him, I never had to clean that out), Brothers devised a heinous prank to play.

Tom shooed me to the other end of the head thus separating us from Mol by three or four stools and partitions, so that he could not see us. Tom rolled a wad of toilet paper into a ball the size of a grapefruit and lit the thing with his cigarette lighter. Then he dropped the whole fiery thing into the trough and away it floated. It passed under the unsuspecting Mol's bare ass and other vulnerable fleshy parts. Mol yelped in pain. Brothers ran laughing and hooting from the head. Mol followed, with his pants half up (or half down) slapping his singed ass, in hot pursuit. Literally.

Just once during my tour on the Dione were we subject to, as all ships are, inspection by the the brass from headquarters to determine the ship's seaworthiness and the crew's duty-worthiness. The Dione was paid a visit by a group called Eastern Area Inspectors. They were former ships' captains and other experts in the naval arts. Their mission certified the ship was seaworthy and her crew duty-worthy. Such inspections are often conducted at sea with the crew at General Quarters. This inspection was conducted at sea, at Battle Stations, as an ASW (anti-submarine warfare) maneuver.

During this particular inspection, my Battle Station was the K-Gun. Both were mounted starboard and port on the aft quarter. The K-Gun was a WW II vintage depth charge rack. It shoots a fifty-five-gallon drum loaded with explosives about one hundred yards off ship. When the drum hits the water, hopefully the ship is several hundred yards down the line. When the charge reaches it's pre-set depth, it explodes sending a great geyser of water into the air well behind the ship, which is now even further out of harm's way. My duty was communications with the bridge (fire control), on the sound power phones. I wore a headset and microphone. The K-Gun was operated by a Gunnery Mate whom I told to fire and cease fire per the bridge (fire control).

The Gunnery Mates were supervised by the Gunnery Officer. He decided that for this inspection he would set and cock the charge himself. He did so. The order came down from the bridge (fire control) to "fire K-Gun #1."

"Fire #1!" I yelled.

The mate tugged the firing lanyard. Instead of shooting fifty feet up and one hundred yards out, the damn thing just rolled off the rack and into the sea. It rattled along the side of the ship, slowly sinking. Everyone on deck looked at each other, then over the rail, then back at each other.

A collective, "Oh shit!" sent every man high-tailing it for the bow to get as far away as possible. As if the bow could be far enough away from anything like that. I could hear the charge clanging against the hull as I made my way to the bow. Just short of reaching it, the charge detonated and the stern of the ship left the water. Damage control reported the propeller gone, taking on water below deck, and the lazzerette unrecognizable. Even with full pumps, she was just afloat. Luckily, the Coast Guard Cutter Iris out of Galveston was nearby on maneuvers and came to our rescue by towing us in to her home port for repairs.

This would have been far less believable if we had not shortly before fired the forward 3-inch-50 taking our own jack staff off the bow. This was the kind of stuff inspectors lived for. And there was more. Tom Brothers was the hot shell man on the gun that day. He was responsible for dealing with the hot ejected shell casing. When the damn thing was fired, taking out the jack staff, the shell ejected and Tom wasn't paying attention, as usual. The hot shell ejected out of the breech right through Brothers' hands and hit the third loader dead square in the forward. He was still out cold when we all ran from the depth charge to the bow.

Even though the Dione had a reputation for mishaps, they were not always the fault of us junior pukes. Sometimes the officers were spacing out on their own, like the depth charge incident. Even Mickey Mouse could mess up and I loved it when he did.

Coming into the base at Galveston, Mickey was at the helm piloting the ship into dock. At this dock all the ships were parked parallel except for a few at the very back end, which had their sterns to the dock. Mickey entered the harbor at a good clip and neglected to slow the ship until well past the outer marker.

When he called "slow to 1/3," it was already too late. The crew who had assembled on the forward deck were at attention as the ship came along the dock. They began to grumble as it became apparent that Mr. Merrit was about to overshoot the Dione's berth.

"Better slow her, Sir," someone hollered up to the bridge, over the serious discussion the Captain was having with Mickey regarding his piloting skills.

"All back 1/3," the XO commanded. Nothing happened to our forward speed and the old Dione began to vibrate.

"All back 2/3's," Mickey demanded. As the ship approached its berth it became evident that we were not only going to overshoot it, but we were on a full collision course for a thirty-six-foot unsinkable lifeboat that two Coasties were painting. They say those lifeboats are unsinkable because they will right themselves after capsizing. The ship began to vibrate more.

"All back full!" Mickey screamed. The two Coasties jumped ship, paint cans into the water, they were over the side. Now the ship began to growl under the strain from such a reversal of forces. Guys were having trouble standing up. The Dione's bow clove the unsinkable lifeboat. It sank right there beside the dock, further field-testing it. Mickey stopped, before crossing another "T."

Soon after, I was sated of the Dione and her crew. I saw no future in painting, scraping or depth charging. I had to get off. I started applying for the numerous and sundry schools the Coast Guard offered.

It was not until years later that I learned from several reliable sources in the Coast Guard that the Dione was considered the misfit repository for the 8th Coast Guard district, which encompasses Mobile, Alabama to Matemoras, Mexico. I guess the brass figured if they put all the screwups on one ship at least the damage would be confined to a small and specific area. They were right, because there were plenty of screwups and damage was done.

PART II

PART II

By 1958, I had spent my first year breaking in the Coast Guard, only to incur the exact opposite result. I concluded, through extensive and exhausting research, that the deck force aboard a Coast Guard Cutter was not a position I intended to hold through my entire enlistment. I was not a model seaman. I had no skills, so my options were limited without some further schooling. I at least had enough sense to recognize that fact.

Radio school was my savior in that regard. But after graduation in Groton, Connecticut my soaring spirit was bureaucratically swatted back to earth by reassignment to the 8th Coast Guard District and the Dione's sister ship, the USCGC Nike. Despite the mythological speed of its godly namesake, the Nike was not. Like her sister, the Nike managed a generous twelve knots in a following sea. She carried limited fresh water allowing for one shower every twelve days. While I was on her, she took a fifty-seven degree roll in thirty-foot Gulf seas. I did not like shipboard duty - I damn sure didn't like that fifty-seven degree roll.

I continued my efforts at furthering my education and skills by acceptance into AL School (aviation electronics school). AL school made me into a flying radioman. I attended in Elizabeth City, North Carolina. It was an uneventful stint. I applied myself and had no time for shenanigans. This slight change in my skills and knowledge would lead me to the love of my life - flying.

One Saturday after applying for everything the Coast Guard had to offer, I received orders to report to Sonar School in New Orleans, for a ping test. Sunday, the Coast Guard gave me a Greyhound bus ticket to New Orleans, but no per diem. I was broke.

Before I left the Dione, Chief Patterson expressed his heartfelt remorse to see me leave the ship. I asked the Chief if I could speak off the record and he said yes. So I told him he was the most miserable son-of-a-bitch I had ever met and if I ever met him again, I would love to kick his ass. The Chief said it would probably be in my best interest not to meet him again. And with that I was off the Dione and on my way to Sonar School. So I thought.

The ping test is to determine if the applicant has the audio dexterity and acuity to hear well enough to operate sonar and distinguish the various pitches and sounds attendant to that duty. On the way down to New Orleans I caught what might still be the worst head cold I have ever had.

On Monday, which was test day, I took the ping test and failed it miserably. Hell, I couldn't hear a damn thing. The testing officer said it was the lowest test score ever. So they gave me the test again and I did only slightly better this time scoring ten correct instead of my previous three out of 150. The testing officer said I couldn't go to Sonar School. I begged him to give me a few days to let my head cold clear then test me again. He flatly refused, "no," and they would have to "send me somewhere else, 'cause I wasn't going to sonar school."

I was disappointed to say the least, but took solace in the fact that I was being transferred off the Dione. That afternoon I stopped at the personnel office to inquire where I would be sent, only to be told that the place in greatest need of seamen was the 8th Coast Guard district and specifically the USCGC Dione. The room started spinning and I damn near passed out. I begged, cajoled and pleaded with the personnel officer to find me another berth, but to no avail. The next day I boarded a Greyhound bus back to Freeport and the Dione. It surely was the shortest, most miserable ride of my life. I only now realized how fast a Greyhound bus can be. I arrived in Freeport about noon on Wednesday. I had been gone all of four days.

As I walked the gangway to board the ship, Chief Patterson happened to be on deck and greeted me with great guffaws of laughter and a frightening glint in his eye. Clearly he intended to make me pay for voicing my opinion of him only four days earlier. Needless to say, I began what turned out to be the month from hell as I was assigned every shit detail imaginable and some unimaginable. After what seemed to be the mid-term of a life sentence, I received orders to report for Radio School. I didn't particularly want Radio School, but it just happened to be one of the courses I had put in for and it was a means to an end - getting off the Dione and away from Chief Patterson.

Shortly after receiving my orders I was on my way to Groton, Connecticut, arriving there in the late fall - just before Halloween. Groton is a beautiful New England town with lots of trees and grass, and the only oyster shells I was likely to see would be on my plate. It would be the first time I had ever seen the leaves change and fall. The base is anchored by an old New England sea town mansion overlooking the Thames River, directly across from New London where the Coast Guard Academy is. This place was more like a college campus than a military installation. Numerous schools were housed there. Heaven compared to the dank and rank old girl that the Dione was. Actual flush toilets and you could sleep without any part of your body touching steel.

I was assigned a room with three other guys. Of those only Perry Chighizola is memorable. Everybody called him " Chico," so he said. He was from Grand Isle, Louisiana. Oyster shells again. There was another guy called Bitner, who was some distant heir to the Kodak fortune, he called his parents Art and Ruth.

It wasn't long before we had Saturday night passes and found ourselves across the river in New London, drinking at the Seven Brothers bar. Chico could *drink.* Bitner's efforts to keep up led to his utter inebriation. He got drunk so fast that Chico and I had to put him in a cab back to the base. We continued to drink, and to entertain ourselves we played pool for a local bar-girl's favor. I think she was drunker than us, because she agreed to be the prize. The game was probably the longest one on record due to our blood alcohol levels but we managed to finish and damned if I recall who was the winner. I only remember that the girl bore a striking resemblance to Chief

Patterson, which was enough to send me packing, Chico in pursuit.

I'm still really not sure how we made it back to the base, but once there the alcohol took over again so we decided to sneak in, even though we didn't need to. We could have just walked in the gate and probably been escorted to bed, tucked in by some understanding Chief. But no, we *had* to sneak in. We scaled the fence and of course set Security after us. It's always been funny to me, the way a drunk is able to elude his pursuers. We ran like hell, hid and eluded them, finding ourselves in front of a house with an enormous jack-o'lantern on the porch. We took it back to our room and set it up, lending a homey atmosphere to the stark barracks' accommodations.

The next morning I awoke with the penance of the night before stuck to my hair and smelling like the floor of the Seven Brothers. I was greeted by the moans and groans of Chico and Bitner and the sneering jack-o'lantern. Our first thoughts after how bad we felt were of evidence-disposal. We knew we would be on extra duty if anybody saw the pumpkin and it was far too big to disguise or walk out of the building with. Chico suggested we cut it up into small pieces and stuff the pieces into our peacoat pockets. We couldn't get much in a pocket. The thing was so damn big. It took the better part of Sunday morning, making trips between our room and every dumpster and trash can on the base to disperse it so no one could tell where it came from.

Later that day an announcement regarding the theft of the CO's jack-o'lantern was broadcast over the base P.A. We were lucky that night.

Chico was ever the prankster. A Coonass from Louisiana. He said, "A Coonass, cher, is somebody who can stand in forty acres of rice and tell you how much gravy that's gon' take," He resembled a very hairy fire-plug and talked with the sing-song cadence so common to his home. "Hey Smitty, wha' for you did 'dat?" he would ask.

Knowing that I would leave the Coast Guard when my hitch was up, I looked for some other educational opportunities while at Groton. There were many to choose from but for some reason, I selected a correspondence course in muscular therapy. God knows what I was thinking but it wasn't about staying in the Coast Guard. The course came with an instructional manual, some powders and oils for massage work. What was I thinking? The manual suggested that you practice on your family members and friends. What *was* I thinking - muscular therapy at Coast Guard base? Reluctantly, Chico and the other guys agreed to endure my practice massage sessions. One night just before tattoo, which is the warning prior to lights out, I was practicing massage techniques on Chico with the book open on the table between the set of bunks. Chico was on a lower bunk. I had his hairy back pretty well oiled and was manipulating his back muscles like the book said. Jeez, that guy was hairy. Whenever he went without a shirt, someone would query, "Hey man ain't you hot with that sweater on?"

Deep in the concentration of practicing my new trade, I completely missed tattoo and the lights suddenly went out. So I stepped back off Chico's bunk to retrieve my book and trade paraphenalia. I must have made some noise by bumping into the table in the dark because the door flew open and the light flashed on. When the night security guy stepped in, Chico seized the opportunity by springing from his bunk to complain.

"Hey man, 'dis guy was rubbing all over me in my bunk, you gotta do sumtin' 'bout 'dis. Every night he get in my bunk and rub all over me."

The guard looked me over with a skeptical eye while Chico continued.

"Hey Smitty, what for you do 'dat, every night man?" Back to the guard Chico said, "They tryin' to break him a 'dat."

Now there I was, standing in my underwear, clutching a book, some powder and oil, trying to explain to the guard that I was practicing my correspondence course.

The guard shook his head and said I had to go with him to the OD's office. Of course everybody in the barracks was peeking out their door as I walked down the hall to the OD's office still clutching my book and unguents. I was the same way in front of the OD, who was filling out a report on my deviant behavior with another seaman when Chico and the other guys came in to 'fess up that it was all a joke. The report went on my record anyway. As I walked the hall back to my room, the barracks erupted with cat-calls and whistles and request for backrubs. That ended my muscular therapy career.

Radio school itself involved learning to type as well as take and send code. Just about everyone else could already type. I couldn't and consequently had to learn code and typing at the same time. I could take code faster than I could type, which caused me some problems. While taking code, I always fell behind a couple of sentences on the typewriter. During the mid-term exam the typewriter ran out of paper. I was already so far behind that I couldn't stop to reload the thing, so I just kept typing the code on the roller of the machine. When time was called, I had to hand in my paper and the typewriter. The proctors actually graded my test off the roller and I passed. They must have needed radiomen real bad.

Often during the six months at Groton and despite the intensity of school, we could get weekend passes. Frequently, I used mine to go to different places around the state and sometimes up to Hartford. One trip up to Hartford, I met a guy named Lonnie Tomerlin - a student in ET school, who offered to show me around New York, the next time I had a pass. I had made the trip several times before but figured it would be great to have somebody show me around, so I took Lonnie up on his offer. He seemed like a good enough guy but I warned him that I was in the Coast Guard and really did not have any disposable income. He said that was O.K. because he would get us some money in New York. We took the train to New York. Well, I didn't know this until we got to New York, but Lonnie's idea of getting the money involved rolling gay men by luring them into the bathroom of a gay bar and frightening them into handing over the cash.

Once there, he lead me into a gay bar on the premise of having a starter beer. We bellied up and ordered a couple of cold ones. I noticed we were getting some serious eyeball from a couple of other gentlemen seated at the other end of the bar. Lonnie flirted back a little. After a few minutes of this, through eye and hand signals he and one of the guys went to the men's room, while I uncomfortably ignored the smiles of the other gentlemen. I waited and I waited. Finally the guy Lonnie went off with came back to rejoin his friend. Lonnie did not return. I went back to the men's room to see what is keeping Lonnie only to find him out cold, slumped over the toilet with his tie jerked around backwards and his hat in the bowl. Lonnie was not a big guy and the other gentlemen was smaller than me. I figured I could confront him. When I returned to the bar this guy jumped up to ask me if I "want some of that too?" I declined, grabbed up Lonnie and never returned to New York.

GULFPORT

Finally, Radio School was over despite my typing skills and I found myself a Radioman 3rd Class, assigned back to the 8th Coast Guard district, on the USCGC Nike. The Nike was the Dione's sister ship, built around 1929 and the running shoe was not named after her either, considering she topped out at twelve knots, just like the Dione. Man, these people were just not cooperating with me on this deal.

The Nike performed many and frequent two-week Gulf of Mexico and Gulf of Campeche patrols, for smugglers and search and rescue. The Nike tied up right downtown in Gulfport, Mississppi. The best thing about Gulfport was Biloxi. I lived on the ship. Conditions on the Nike were close. The crew slept in multiple-tier sea hammocks, swinging canvas bunk beds. They afforded all but enough room to blink. You had to get out of the hammock to turn over or else bump the man above or below. Bumps in the night were not well received. People got sick in them at sea and soiled their mates. It was hot and without air conditioning. It was sticky and showerless. One shower per man per fourteen-day patrol or every twelve days. It was uncomfortable and nasty. The rate of Radioman was not much better than Seaman Apprentice but it wasn't deck hand.

During one stay in port at the dock in downtown Gulfport, the ship was tied up almost next to the new "Aquatarium" the city planned to dedicate. Some how the Nike became an ancillary part of the festivities by opening her deck for tours. Prior to the official ribbon-cutting ceremony at the "Aquatarium," a movie actress of great beauty and significant renown had agreed to tour the Nike. At the appointed time, the limo arrived and out stepped the actress to begin her ascent of our gangway.

I was on the bridge along with the Quarter Master and another seaman or two. The Quarter Master thought it would be cute to announce the actress' arrival with a comment over the intercom to the berthing decks below. He flipped the intercom switch for the berthing compartment and put the mic to his mouth. He winked at me. While he winked, one of the seamen flipped the switch to the bull-horn position.

The Quarter Master announced to the berthing deck (and to the rest of the world within a quarter mile), in the worst possible terms that only a sailor could conjure, to describe the pulchritude represented by the actress' presence onboard.

"Attention below decks, we got @#$*&! onboard," he blurted before realizing he was on bull-horn. I am sure the announcement was heard in the "Aquatarium" lobby.

The actress stopped dead in her tracks about halfway to the Nike's gunnels, and raised her hand, middle finger extended, in a gesture of utter contempt. She gave the finger over her head all the way down the gangway back to her limo. She turned while standing in the limo door and gave the ship and all on it one more good stiff one. The tour was over.

PART III

PART III

My 1959 graduation from AL School gave me the great satisfaction of knowing I would be an aviator. I would fly. I would not chip and paint on the deck of some other century military vessel. I was a brand new AL3 (Aviation Electronicsman 3rd Class). I was also assigned back to to the 8th Coast Guard District, but this time in Corpus Christi, Texas. There I became intimate with the workhorse of Coast Guard aviation, the HU-16 Albatross. Affectionately (or otherwise) known as the "Goat." You could always tell a "Goat" flyer by the frequent use of his two favorite words - "huh?" and "what?" both indicative utterances of the deaf.

Corpus was the southern most air station in the 8th District. From there we patrolled the length and breadth of the Gulf, to the very edge of Mexican territorial waters just twelve miles off its coast. I spent many happy hours developing my love affair with aviation in Corpus Christi.

From Corpus I was assigned to Kodiak, Alaska. Assignment to Kodiak was one of those significant moments that one fails to recognize. I arrived there in the Spring of 1961, via a two-week stay in the Whidby Island Naval Hospital, which was the resulting effect of totaling two cars on the drive up. Oh! My wife decided en route that she and our 9-month-old daughter would stay in San Diego and seek a divorce. She did not want to live in Kodiak despite the fact that our newly purchased household full of furnishings was on its way to Alaska - talk about a significant moment.

The fact of the matter is that the Coast Guard could not have sent me to a better place at that time in my life. It was a sportsman's paradise. The base athletic curriculum was a jock's paradise as well. I couldn't get enough of it all - hunting, fishing, flying, beach combing and all the sports I could endure. I helped the Coast Guard Air Station win the Captain's Cup from our Navy hosts, which resulted in free trips off the Island to the All-Navy Competition. The flying was the best - any other flying duty in the world paled by comparison. In 1961 we were flying HU-16's, C-123's (which were just big gliders with two engines) and H-13 Bell Helicopters. We flew the Bell off the cutter Storis and the ice-breaker Northwind. I thought I had lived - until my first nighttime water landing to pick up some drunk native who lied about his injury (if there even was one), so he could go to town for the weekend.

After three years and the Good Friday earthquake of 1964, I left Kodiak for San Diego. I had decided to stay in the Coast Guard and my best opportunity for advancement was to apply for Officer Candidate School. In San Diego I dedicated myself to gaining acceptance into OCS. To start with I had to lose forty-five pounds. I had only seven weeks in which to accomplish this feat and still be considered for the next class. There were only two per year and I didn't want to wait for another year.

I played handball for an hour every night at the YMCA in a full wet-suit. And I played basketball for an hour the same way, except with just the wetsuit top. By the fourth day of the sixth week I had lost forty-seven pounds and failed the flight physical due to high blood pressure. The Navy Flight Surgeon was the coolest cucumber I ever met. He had me come back the next day and take a nap. While I napped he took my blood pressure and I passed.

Finally, I was off to OCS in Yorktown, Virginia to begin my metamorphosis, if not completely then at least partially. OCS was not tougher, just a lot more fun than boot camp. Somehow I successfully graduated from OCS and was sent to the Coast Guard Air Station, Miami - at Dinner Key. There I was the not-so-perfect ensign, waiting for my slot to open up in flight training at Naval Air Station, Pensacola. It was as if they had been waiting for me at Dinner Key. For during the two months of temporary duty, every practical joke and trick imaginable was played on me. Despite my mates' proclivity and penchant for making me the butt of their pranks, it was the beginning of some wonderful relationships that would last my whole career - and beyond. I don't recall that I have ever gotten even with the likes of Billy Ed Murphy and George Kreitmeyer for the torment they perpetrated on me at Dinner Key.

By the end of 1965 I was off to flight school. I couldn't believe it, nor I think could anyone else.

The flights were mostly routine out of Corpus but something would always happen to spice them up a little bit. One day we launched as usual and were airborne for about thirty minutes when the door to the nose section of the HU-16 "Goat" opened and Stanley A. Tuttle emerged from the nose compartment. He was not assigned to this flight crew. I had no idea why he was onboard until he explained.

It seems that Stanley A. Tuttle, was a wee tad reluctant in his embarrassment to come out of the compartment when the engines woke him. He was in enough shit for sleeping on duty without getting caught in the act. Stanley A. decided that there was a good chance the plane was only being taxied to another spot on the ramp. If that was so, he could get out when the taxi pilot shut down and left the aircraft. It was not until he heard the engines run up for takeoff that he realized his mistake. After thirty or so minutes the unheated nose compartment temperature helped Stanley A. to overcome his embarrassment and come forth - aft, actually.

Another notable comrade from those early days of my aviation career was LT Bill Hunter. He was, without a doubt, the oldest Lieutenant in the Coast Guard. He switched services in his mid to late forties. He came over to the Coast Guard from the Army Air Corps where he was a pilot, a damn fine pilot - one hell of an old-school aviator, seat of the pants, dead reckoning kind of flyer. Intrepid may fall short as a single word description. Mr. Hunter was also the Supply Officer.

One night I sat in my usual Radioman seat, behind Mr. Hunter in the pilot seat. The engines of our HU-16 purred at idle while Mr. Hunter grew exponentially more impatient with each passing minute that our co-pilot was late.

"Where the hell is that son-of-a-bitch?" he fumed.

He fidgeted with switches and knobs and in his seat. Finally he half turned to me and yelled over the com set.

"I don't need that son-of-a-bitch to fly this thing. Smith, get up here - in the other seat and put that headset on. I just need to slide by the tower. Get up here," he ordered.

I hesitated for a moment. The whole idea didn't really appeal to me. Hell, you weren't supposed to fly those things without two pilots. What if something happened to Mr. Hunter in flight? Who would fly it then? I didn't like it. No sir, not one bit.

"Smith get up here."

Reluctantly, I did. We taxied past the tower and to the end of the runway for takeoff. Just as Mr. Hunter swung the plane around, a car pulled up and out jumped the co-pilot. I think Mr. Hunter would have gone with me in the front seat.

One day shortly after my first stint as co-pilot, I was on the hangar deck when a disheveled gentleman of advanced years approached with the inquisitive stroll of a man looking for something. I intercepted him about midway across the hangar deck to see if I could help him. Surely he was lost. What business could such an apparent vagabond have in a Coast Guard aircraft hangar?

"No," he said. "Don't need no hep' young fella. Jus' need to see Bill Hunter."

I led him back to the area were Mr. Hunter's office was. He wasn't in and one of the other supply guys asked if he could help.

"No," he said. "Need to see Bill, I guess."

The supply guy explained that Mr. Hunter would not return for some time, as he was flying.

"Well, maybe you can hep' me then," he said. "I come fer my jackit."

"Beg your pardon, Sir?" the supply guy responded.

"One 'a them flight jackits, the leather ones. Bill's a friend of mine from down to the Amurican Leejun, en he said I could have one them leather jackits. An' 'tother night down to the Leejun he said a new batch come in, en he'd git me one. Well I'm goin' on vacation tomorra en I wanted to git that jackit."

Jaws dropped and all the supply guys stood dumfounded.

"We don't really give those out to the general public, sir. Those are for flight crews," said the supply guy.

"Well, everybody else down to the Leejun done got theirs," he complained. Flies buzzed in and out of the open mouths.

LCDR Carl Scott was a great guy unless you pissed him off. Then he would become intolerable and insufferable. One day after a long flight, Carl was not in the best of moods. It only became fouler when we were assigned the administrative task of updating new pages to the Station's

Communications Books. The Com Books told us how to communicate in code and other classified communications information necessary in flight. They were comprised of hundreds of pages. There were five copies. One in the OPS Center and one in each of four aircraft. Every so often the books would be updated with new pages or changes to pages. It was all very classified and because we had the security clearances, Carl and I got the duty.

The whole process had a meticulous order that ensured the accuracy of the update. For example, we would replace all the page #2's in each book with a new #2. Then the old #2's would go in a pile and be checked off the inventory list. This process continued on through many hundreds of pages until all the new pages are installed and the pile of old pages matches the inventory list. It took hours to complete, but finally the mind-numbing task was over. I asked Carl what we should do with all the old pages.

"Throw 'em in the trash basket," he said without thinking.

Without thinking, I did just that and we left for the night, exhausted from our day of flight and mind-altering paperwork.

The next morning Carl Scott greeted me with a smile and a good-natured demeanor.

"Where did you put those Com Book pages, Smitty?" he asked.

"In the trash can, like you said," I replied.

He looked in all the wastebaskets, but each was empty. That's when he went ballistic. "How stupid of a son-of-a-bitch" was I is what he wanted to know. My reply was, "Only as stupid as per your instructions, sir!" The quip only exacerbated his foul mood.

It took a few minutes but we finally determined that the cleaning staff had been through early, before our arrival. The Com Book pages were in the dumpster outside the OPS Center. Carl was beside himself with both relief and anger. The pages were classified material and required submittal to headquarters for proper inventory and shredding - the relief part was that they were still in the dumpster, the anger part was that they were inside a dumpster full of God-knew-what.

Carl did not get in the dumpster. I spent the entire morning rummaging the contents to find all the old pages. Every time I handed Carl a page he would check it off the list and call me a stupid son-of-a-bitch.

"Yes, sir" was all I could say and hand him another page.

"You are the stupidest son-of-a-bitch I ever saw."

"Yes, sir."

There wasn't one page out of all the hundreds I plucked from the depths that didn't have some kind of goo, smear or slime on it and there wasn't one page that he didn't call me a stupid son-of-a-bitch when he took it from me. And then one more time, when I clamored out of the dumpster.

I was, however, smart enough to make the Base softball team. LCDR Paul "Pierre" Smith was the pitcher. I caught him. He was an excellent hurler and threw the softball like an eight-pound cannon shot. Many times after a game I was required to ice my mitt hand down before it would work properly. On this day we were pitted against the Marines attached to the base. This day Paul Smith threw with additional vigor - after all we were playing against Jarheads.

He threw so hard that the Marines were hitless and we won the game. Impressed with our play and out of good sportsmanship, the Marines invited us to lunch. We had to accept. It would have been rude to do otherwise. After the game, my hand - already sensitive from a season of stopping his projectiles - hurt like the dickens, but I didn't get the opportunity to ice it down. Our hosts awaited. The Marine Exchange was adjacent to their barracks, hence two hundred jarheads were seated when we entered.

I bought a sandwich and a half-pint of chocolate milk. It was difficult to find a table with all those guys already dining but we did. The Coastie softball team sat down at a table in an a sea of khaki and burr-heads. I opened my milk and set it on the table while I massaged my hand a little and complained to Paul. He told me to shut up and quit whining. That's when I picked up the milk with my bad hand and shook it.

I was sure that I had the open end pinched shut, but my damaged hand couldn't tell what it was doing. I held the carton just above my head and shook like hell. Chocolate milk sloshed through the air. Marines on all points of the compass were doused two and three deep, all the way around our table. The room went silent. All eyes had been on the Coasties - what were they doing here? We had just trounced their team and the atmosphere in the room was already a bit less than affable. They all stood, all two hundred. I paid for cleaning for about twelve sets of khakis and not with my life. Man, those Jarheads were sore.

My life did take a change for the better when Master Chief John Timmons took an interest in me. Chief Timmons was a great guy but like any Chief, you did not trifle with him. He was the Master-at-Arms in charge of all the cleanup duties. Among those were the heads in the hangar. They were located on both the first and second level office suites. The Master-at-Arms does not have the time or inclination to actually perform the cleanup duties, so delegation is the key to getting the job done. That's where I came in, as enlisted meat for the grinder.

"Smitty, I got a little assignment for ya!" he told me one day.

"What is it, Chief?"

He explained to me that by way of report and personal inspection, he had discovered someone was wiping boogers on the stall partition wall of the head - next to the toilet paper dispenser. It seriously pissed the Chief off. Someone was messing with his heads. Nobody messed with Master Chief Timmons. He assigned me the task of catching the culprit.

"I want you to catch that nose-pickin' son-of-a-bitch," he ordered.

"Beg pardon Chief, but just how am I gonna do that?" I whined.

"By cleaning those heads, is how."

Clean them I did, regularly, daily and sometimes twice. I cleaned them at the end of each duty section's watch and in the middle of a watch. This was no easy feat as I had other duties. Some days I operated the radio in flight. Some days, guys were flying when I cleaned. It was hard to tell who was doing what in those heads. And really, did I want to know? Well, that's what the Chief was paying me for. Gradually, a process of elimination developed more from the repetitive arts than from the deductive ones. I was able to narrow the culprit to one particular duty section of three possible candidates. I did, however, manage to deduce that the culprit was left-handed by the position of the booger. I did this by sitting on the stool of a desecrated stall and discovered that one just couldn't wipe a booger next to the TP holder, unless one were left-handed. This was a great boost to my investigative confidence and I vowed to pursue the cad to his booger-wiping end.

And then, by the complete happenstance that so often accompanies sheer perseverance, I caught the guy red-handed. I had just come in from a routine flight when I thought it prudent to check the heads. They were a mess. It was the end of my watch and time for the next duty section to take over. I noticed that many of the guys from that section were already in the hangar. It was the suspect duty section.

I ran, still in my flight suit to the cleaning locker, grabbed my supplies and raced back to clean the heads. I scrubbed and polished. I also checked by the toilet paper dispenser in each stall - on both the first and second level office suites - nothing , no boogers anywhere. I was dejected. I picked up the wastecan from the first-floor head on the hangar deck and took it out to the dumpster. As I opened the head door to leave with the basket in my hand, a guy from the offending duty section came through it. I walked to the dumpster keeping the head door in my view the entire time. As I came back to the head door the same guy was leaving. I noticed that he wore a watch on his right wrist. He was left-handed. No one else had entered during this time span.

Quickly, I checked each stall. Bingo! Middle stall - big nasty one glommed to the partition wall next to the TP holder. Yes! Got him. I ran like a little tattletale to the Chief who was just leaving the hangar. I broke the news with pride and satisfaction while pointing to the guy.

"That nose-pickin' son-of-a-bitch," The Chief said as he walked toward the man.

Chief Timmons was grateful thereafter and he showed it by assigning the culprit to clean the heads until further notice. In fact that same guy was still cleaning the heads when I left for another duty station, a year later. You just don't trifle with the Chief and thereafter, he assigned me the good duty, for the rest of my tour. The culprit was one of the mechanics from the offending duty section. Guess what the nickname for mechanics is - "Nose Pickers."

Matamoras, Mexico is not a place that any serviceman will return from with even the semblance of military decorum. Such was the case when LT Billy Ed Murphy, Chico and myself paid a visit to that legendary of all border towns. We left Chico to his own devices as we had an early mission the next day. Billy Ed and I worked our way back to the border in an inebriated stumble. It had rained during our evening devoted to mass consumption of excellent Mexican food and God only knows how much alcohol. The streets were wet and muddy. The side street we strolled along was lined with open door cribs - dirt floor hovels intended for one purpose only and we were beyond it. As we passed an open door, a woman bailing out her domicile, adroitly sloshed a large bucket of mudwater all over Billy Ed. He was soaked from head to toe.

By the time we arrived at the border checkpoin,t Billy Ed was a complete disgrace to his uniform. His clothing and coat were soaked and covered with mud. He walked the best he could considering his condition (our condition), but it was difficult because his khaki trouser cuffs now sagged under the weight of the mudwater they contained. It caused them to flap under his heels with each step he took. This only stretched them out further and pulled them lower on his waist until his dishevelment could be considered out of uniform.

Besides the allowable bottle of liquor that he carried in his hand, Billy Ed had an illicit bottle of contraband liquor in the armpit of his coat. So loose was Billy Ed, that when addressed by the Customs Agent he immediately stiffened to attention and saluted, loosening the armpit grip on his contraband. The bottle crashed on the pavement at his feet, covering them and the agents with a shiny film of booze.

"Are you drunk sailor?" asked the Customs Agent while shaking the liquor off his shoes.

"No sshhir, but I used to be," chortled Billy Ed, straight-faced and still holding his salute.

The Customs Agent let us enter the U.S. but only with the proviso that Billy Ed was in my custody. This seemed quite amusing to me that the Agent released Billy Ed, the Lieutenant, into the custody of me, a 3rd Class.

Finally back at the hotel, we quietly shuffled down the hall to our rooms. I leaned him against the door to the room he shared with our Aircraft Commander while he fumbled for his key - khakis still dripping mudwater - cuffs tucked under the heels of his shoes. My room was adjacent and as I unlocked my door, I heard Billy Ed say, "Oh, Goo Mooring Caap'n."

Captain Owen Siler was already up, showered, shaved and dressed. There stood LT Murphy in his mud-encrusted khakis, hungover and clutching a bottle of booze. I quietly closed my door to get ready for the day.

Later that day while flying the Gulf Coast around Port Sulphur with Captain Siler, Billy Ed and I suffered horribly from the ravages of overindulgence. There was no containing our gas. Soon the entire aircraft was filled with the vapors of penitent men. Billy Ed looked over at Captain Siler from the co-pilots seat and pricked his nose in the air. "Whoo-wee Captain, those sulphur refineries sure do stink today," he said, smiling back to me in the radio seat.

Captain Siler, along with many others, would continue to reappear throughout my career. Two such were Chico and Bitner, my roommates at Radio School in Groton. Both were stationed in Biloxi while I was in Corpus. Occasionally we would meet somewhere, when liberty or weekends allowed. On time we met in New Orleans for Mardi Gras. We spent several glorious days in the pursuits of revelry. By the time we parted for our individually long drives home, me to Corpus - they to Biloxi, we were exhausted and probably had no business operating a pair of scissors, let alone a motor vehicle. I know I was tired.

Several days after returning to Corpus, I called to see if they made it home O.K. and tell them what a great time I had, only then to find out they had encountered a problem on the return trip and were both in the hospital. In short order I located them and called their hospital room. Bitner answered the phone.

They were tired alright and in their exhausted state with Chico behind the wheel, they had run off the end of a missing bridge that spanned a canal. The bridge, out for whatever reasons, had already claimed another vehicle only moments before. It lay at the bottom of the canal some twenty-six feet below the road surface. It had taken out the barrier and warning flasher. When Chico and Bitner approached in the dark and fog, they had no idea a bridge was there, or rather, not there. They simply sailed off the end into open space. Their vehicle landed on top of the poor slob in the first vehicle. Binter broke both his arms and Chico his neck.

"Are you guys gonna be alright?" I asked.

"Oh yeah!" said Bitner. "But Mal, I gotta tell you. While we were airborne and Chico had a death grip on the steering wheel, he says, 'Hey man, give me full flaps and 2300.' Can you believe that?"

Full flaps and 2300 are the settings for landing a "Goat" just before touch down. Chico and Bitner were later discharged from the Coast Guard due to the nature of their injuries. Chico sued the State of Louisiana and won. With the settlement, he bought himself a small grocery store at Grand Isle and his folks a shrimp boat.

Like Captain Siler, I would encounter Chico again many years later.

THE PIG AND THE GOAT

The Bay of Campeche again - Hell still. It was a little better this time, but only just. When I made the Campeche patrols before on the Dione and the Nike, they were twelve days long, dock to dock. I thought the Campeche patrols were the worst thing I had ever experienced and they were the driving force behind my desire to get off the Dione. I thought Aviation Electronics School would get me off the Nike and away from the Bay of Campeche. There I was again flying over the damn thing. Graduation from Aviation Electronics School at Elizabeth City had landed me an assignment to Corpus Christi, headquarters for Campeche Air Patrols.

In those days, the work horse of the Campeche Air Patrol was the HU-16 Albatross. Those patrols were my first introduction to the "Goat." Those "Goat" rides were between eleven and twelve hours in duration - or was that endure-ation. Either way it is a great deal of time to spend flying over water, in an oil drum with wings, without air conditioning, that smelled like a refinery inside and to the occupants sounded and felt like someone was beating on it with a baseball bat.

I am not quite sure which was worse, twelve days in the Gulf of Campeche on the Dione or twelve hours over it in a "Goat." It might be a toss up.

So it came to pass that I was about five or six hours into one Campeche patrol. LT Bill Hunter was the AC. We had been flying lines and checking on the U.S. fishing fleet. Mr. Hunter put the rumbling beast into a big sweeping turn over the coast to come around to the next line, when a fire warning light came on for one of the two engines. A "Goat" can fly on one engine but to do so for six hours back to Corpus would be unwise and risky at best. So we - I - declared an emergency over the radio and advised Corpus that we were trying for the dinky and obscure hamlet of Campeche. Bill Hunter was one hell of an aviator and set the thing down light as a feather. No one would have known he was heavy by one engine.

Once on the ground, our flight mechanic trouble shot the problem. He pulled the oil sump drain-plug to find metal shavings in the oil. A sure sign that the engine was done and a replacement would be required for us to fly the "Goat" home. I again advised Corpus over the radio and they responded that we should standby with the aircraft for further instructions. We stood by for several hours in our flight suits sweltering in the unrelenting Campeche sun. We kept ourselves busy disconnecting everything on the engine that we could, but leaving it bolted to the airframe. The installation would go a lot quicker if we were ready when the new engine arrived.

Finally, word came from Corpus to stand down and secure the aircraft. We would have to find accommodations as best we could. It would take ten days for the new engine to arrive. We were flabbergasted - ten days? Why couldn't they just fly one down to us on a C-130? The Mexican government wouldn't allow it was the answer. Relations between Mexico and the U.S. were strained at the time. In fact, this was one of the reasons that we were on Campeche patrol. The Mexican Navy had been confiscating U.S. fishing boats claiming a violation of territorial waters. Diplomatic falderal and red tape would show our engine the long way. It had to clear customs in Mexico City on a commercial carrier before it was shipped to Campeche. We were screwed.

We had no money, no spare clothing, no place to stay. We hitched a ride to the closest big town, which is Merida about fifty miles to the north. There we found the American Consulate and were able to scrounge a loan of $300. There were five guys on the "Goat." Three hundred dollars divided by five over ten days, worked out to $6 per diem - that wasn't much in 1960, not even in Mexico. We went on the hunt for a billet that fit our meager budget.

After some searching, we found a small, but quaint back street (alley) hotel with a cocina y cantina. The owner was delighted to house five men from the U.S. Coast Guard for the next ten days - two meals and one drink included - $250. That took care of the per diem. We had $50 left between us. That night the cocina was excellent and the cantina was lively. We all decided to waste a few pesos on a drink or two.

I awoke the next morning and made my way to the dining room. I found it empty and thought this a bit odd considering the number of guests who had partied in the cantina the previous night, but did not give it a second thought. Because I was the Radioman, it was my responsibility to make the Situation Report (sit rep) to Corpus and to check on the aircraft while I was there. That first day the ninety-minute round trip cab ride cost me a good chunk of our remaining cash. I found the aircraft had been tampered with despite our best efforts at locking it up and a few survival items were missing. I made my report to Corpus and got the news from home - and yes, the engine was still going to take ten days. On the cab ride home I ruminated on our plight. We couldn't afford the expense of the cab ride but I had to contact Corpus every day and check on the aircraft.

The afternoon of the third day our flight suits began to reek. I supposed we could have washed them while we all stood around naked but the thought of wearing flight suits at the beach for seven more days sucked. We found a merchant willing to take our flight suits in exchange for sets of white linen pants and shirts - throw in a straw hat and we had a deal. Now at least we were dressed for the climate. I asked the merchant if there was a cheaper means of getting to Campeche than the local taxi or if he had a car to rent. He had no car to rent, but he knew a man who owned a bus and would some-times rent it. I asked for directions to this man. I made arrangements to rent his bus for a few dollars per day. He would drive.

The next morning I awoke with a new attitude and made my way to the diner-less dining room. Still no breakfasters despite the cantina full of revelers the night before.

"Late sleepers, the guests in this hotel," I thought.

My driver arrived promptly at 8 A.M. and I rode happily to Campeche. On the outskirts of Merida, we came upon a peasant walking his pig along the road. I asked the driver to stop so we could give the man a ride. He did so and I stepped out to help the man and his pig aboard. Once seated he handed me two pesos. One for him and one for his pig. He would ride to Campeche. I accepted. Quickly, I made a deal with the bus driver for ten percent of the fares. We stopped every time we saw some one, collecting centavos and pesos all the way.

We hauled chickens in crates, people in garb like ours, goats, produce, mothers and children. In the ninety minutes it took to drive to Campeche, I made $10 or $12. I was showing a good profit. The aircraft fared less well over the night and more gear was missing. And yes, the engine was still going to take ten days. On the way back we made another $10 or so hauling people, livestock and produce.

That night at dinner, the guys were ebullient over our new-found fortunes. We ate and drank well and it was evident to all in the cantina that our fortunes had changed. It also became evident why there were no diners at breakfast in the morning, when all the women flocked to our table. It was a whorehouse. We were the only permanent residents. No wonder we could get all this for ten days for only $250. They liked us. We got to know the short term residents well - everybody loves Coasties - literally.

While we celebrated, I convinced the house Mariachi band to ride along the next day and play music in the back of the bus. They agreed - for a few dollars. We did even better with the passenger and freight fares. The aircraft was now devoid of anything that wasn't screwed or welded down. And yes, still ten days!

On the last day before the engine arrived, I was riding back to Merida from the aircraft with the Mariachi band playing gaily in the back of the bus. Just outside of Campeche, maybe a mile or so, stood my original passenger, the man with the pig and beside him stood that pig. He waved the bus down and I greeted him warmly and hopped out to assist him and the pig aboard. It was then I noticed the pig's heavily bandaged rear left leg. Actually the left leg was gone and the hip was heavily bandaged. The pig needed a good deal of help ascending the stairs into the bus - hell, what it really needed was that other leg.

I escorted the man and his pig down the aisle to an empty set of seats. The pig got in first and the man took the aisle seat to stretch his legs. I sat in the seat across the aisle.

"I thought the other day when we picked you up, you were taking that pig to market," I said to him.

"No Señor, I go to the wedding of my brother's only daughter. The pig he goes also," he replied.

"But the pig. What's up with the pig?" I went on.

"Oh! Señor, that is a very special pig. When my children were lost in the jungle, this pig, he picked up their scent and lead me to them. When my brother was hurt in his field, the pig rushed to my house and pestered me until I would follow him to my brother. And when a fox tried to raid my chicken house, the pig drove it away. Oh! Señor, this is a very special pig."

"That's all real interesting, but what about the pigs leg? It had four legs last week. What happened to the pig's leg?" I insisted

"As I said, Señor. It was the wedding of my brother's only daughter and I was responsible for the feast. Well, I am a poor man, Señor. I have only this pig. And a pig this special you do not eat all at once."

We did O.K. those ten days. We definitely did better than that pig. Finally the engine arrived and we installed it in our linen whites. We flew back to Corpus in those things and got a good razzing by the other air crews. We only left one guy behind who had been dumb enough to drink the water. They let him out of the hospital about a week later and we picked him up on our next patrol.

That may have been the best of the worst in the Bay of Campeche.

Rotary Cowboy

During my second summer in Kodiak, as an AT2, I was assigned a rather unique job - rounding up elk for the Alaska Division of Fish and Wildlife. Sure, I could do that. I was young and dumb and full of "Semper Par."

Some years earlier a small herd of Roosevelt Elk had been transplanted on Afognak Island, just north of Kodiak. The herd had prospered and done so well that the Division of Wildlife wanted to cull some yearling calves out for transplant to another location in the state. Roosevelt Elk were all but decimated during the early 1900's and this seemed like a good opportunity to re-establish them to their former numbers.

Because the elk to be culled and transplanted were yearlings, the DOW was reluctant to dart them with tranquilizer, for fear of damaging or even killing the animals. So rather than risk the animals' health and life with drugs, we did it the old fashioned way. We ran them down with a helicopter, a small Bell H-13 with plexiglass bubble and skids.

The first step was to spot a likely cow and calf, then cut them out of the herd. Selection was important because a yearling that was too big would prove unmanageable and one too small could be hurt or might not even be weaned. The cow had to be considered as well. Too big was definitely not good. Selection made, we ran them down until the calf tired and became separated from the cow. That's when the chopper pilot came in low alongside the calf and we crewmen jumped out to wrestle it down. It was akin to rodeo bull doggin'. The yearling elk were easy to tire and separate from their mothers, but they were hell to catch.

The damn things wouldn't stand still no matter how tired they were and most of our attempts ended in sore knees and bruised bodies. It is one thing to jump out of a hovering helicopter and quite another to do it atop an already frightened animal. Even a 125-pound yearling elk has an authoritative kick and they had no compunction toward stomping us with sharp hooves. We were ill-attired for such an endeavor and I don't think anything less than chainmail would have sufficed. Aborted attempts found us clinging to the skids as the cow charged under the helicopter. Emergency liftoffs were common. For the most part, we just couldn't get a hold of the damn things, even if the pilot could keep the cow at bay.

On those rare occasions when we actually subdued an animal, it was hog-tied and loaded in the helicopter. Bound and blindfolded, the yearling was fairly easy to transport, which we did immediately to avoid injury - to all. It was taken to a temporary holding pen set up near the settlement of Afognak where a vet would check its condition, inject it with vitamins and draw some blood to make sure the animal was healthy. A DOW officer would tag it and there the DOW staff could feed and care for them while the round up continued, which it did for three months.

We couldn't stress the herd on a daily basis by chasing them with a helicopter so operations were conducted every few days to give the animals (and us), some time to recover. I didn't go on every trip but I did go on most. Some days our efforts yielded only the red and blue imprint of an elk hoof on our bodies. The pilot wasn't getting stomped - I thought about that the whole time. It took all summer to round up twelve head.

After completing my personal lifetime limit of bulldogs from a hovering helicopter (it has to be easier from a horse), we had all the animals penned at Afognak. The time had come to transfer them to another secure area on Annette Island because that's where the Coast Guard Station was at the time. However, there was no holding pen constructed, as they would only stay overnight, before transport to Gravina Island. Gravina is just a short hop across the bay from Annette Island but after the long trip from Kodiak to Annette, both animal and man required overnight billet. Arrangements had been made with a local Indian farmer to use the only fenced field in the immediate vicinity.

Since I had spent the summer and more time than anyone else catching the elk, I was assigned to the transport. After a long day of elk wrangling in a C-123 aircraft, they were safe and secure in the farmer's pen on Annette Island. The next morning they would be off to Gravina.

The Coast Guard Air Station on Annette Island, is not known for its amenities but is known for the Muskeg Lounge. Everybody went to the Muskeg and so did we. It was the Club on base, serving both officers and enlisted. My crew and I were treated well by our hosts on Annette. We reveled there until late. About eleven o'clock that night, a local guy came run-

ning in, yelling to the Captain of the base that twelve of his elk had been
shot. The Captain turned gray because he first thought that twelve of the
many Coasties who were members of the local BPOE, had been shot. Slowly
the realization came that the man was talking about the Afognak yearlings.

The yearlings had escaped their enclosure and were found by the
farmer, happily eating their way through his cabbage patch. He simply
stepped back into his house and returned with a rifle, then methodically shot
them all.

He and his family were skinning and butchering them by the light of
Coleman lanterns when we arrived. As I approached the grizzly scene, a
matronly Indian grandmother stood from her stooped posture over a yearling
elk carcass. The lantern light cast an eerie glisten to her viscera-covered
hands. In one she held a length of intestine. As she blankly stared our way,
the other hand ran the length of the gut between thumb and index finger. Its
contents discharged, speckling her boots. She tossed the gut into a bucket and
turned to resume her posture over the carcass.

I never confirmed the rumor, and only scuttle-butt had the DOW suing
the Coast Guard, the Coast Guard suing the Indian and the Indian suing
them both. The results of which my knowledge is limited only to further
rumor, as follows:

The Indian got to keep the hides and the remaining meat. The DOW
and the Coast Guard were required to split the reimbursement for the value
of the Indian's crop.

Yee - ha!

Seaworthy chevy

The time had come for me to leave Kodiak. A farewell get-together was hastily assembled at the Beach Comber, one of our favorite local watering holes. All my buddies were there to wish me well and send me off to my new duty station. About half way through the evening a local guy I knew rushed over to me while I sat at the bar.

"Hey Mal, what happened to your car?" he asked.

I had a 1954 Chevy Bel Air. An ugly thing it was and suffering from the same degenerative state of rust as most ten-year-old cars living next to the salt. It sported uncountable nicks and dings. I thought the guy was just giving me a little grief about my old beater car, as so many had too often done before.

"Oh! It's always been like that," I replied. He looked at me a little stupidly. I quickly forgot his comment as the evening wore on. When I left to go home some hours later I was confronted by what he meant.

It had been hit and run rear-ended. The trunk and rear fenders were up around the rear window. Its condition reminded me of the old threat "to kick someone's ass up around their shoulders." I walked home that night to the little subdivision of Aluetian Homes. Pollution Homes, we used to call the places. They are still standing today.

The next morning I had the car towed to my house. I really didn't know what to do with it. When I got short and was scheduled to ship out in about a week, I started to get concerned about it. Granted, it was only a $200 car but it was all I had and I would need one in San Diego. I wasn't about to live in San Diego without a car. I had already done that the first seventeen years of my life. No one cared to purchase a badly bent ten-year-old rust bucket and I would not be allowed to put it on a ship in wrecked condition. Now I was out the $200 and couldn't even buy a replacement car in San Diego.

Early one morning about four days before leaving Kodiak, my buddies Victor Bearinger and Bill Matizek showed up at my front door with a Coast Guard stake body truck. In the back of the truck were acetylene torches and a small gasoline welding machine. Bill Matizek was a Metal Smith 1st Class.

"Let's go Smitty," said Vic, bursting through the door at the crack of dawn.

"Where to?"

"We're gonna fix your bucket o' bolts. Just get in the truck."

The sky was just turning pink as we pulled into the Kodiak Police Department's impound lot. The chainlink gate to the unguarded lot lay wildly askew. The KPD could not afford an attendant. This was a self-service impound lot. We drove right in and Bill stopped the truck just feet from another '54 Chevy - a duplicate of mine, except the trunk was were it should be.

Bill made a few measurements and marked the body with a soap stone chalk that all men of the metal arts carry. He fired the torch and within minutes had cut a clean line around the ass end of that Chevy, just behind the rear doors and under the wheel wells, then around under the end of the trunk along the bumper. Bill extinguished the torch and rolled up the hose. He looked for a minute and then hung the hose on the tank valves in the truck bed.

He stepped back to the rear of the Chevy and gave the ass end a good flat kick with the sole of his boot. The whole damn thing shuddered. Bill instructed Vic and I to grab it under the fender wells and lift. It came right off. We put it in the truck and drove to my place. The pink sky was just turning orange.

Back at Pollution Homes, the dim but colorful morning light and the one and a half rusted cars that now adorned my entry, lent a new meaning to the nickname given to my subdivision. Bill repeated the measurements on my car with his soap stone stick. When he fired the acetylene torch and began to cut the back end off on the exact same lines as the impounded car, the image of Pollution Homes became even more apropos.

Bill repeated his technical kick. Vic and I repeated the lift. This time we set the demented ass end of my Chevy down on the ground. We stepped over to the flatbed and lifted the impounded ass end onto my car. Bill fired up the gas welder and spot welded the new ass end in place while Vic and I loaded the demented trunk and fender assembly onto the flat bed. The flashing arc of the welder only intensified my new image of Pollution Homes. We all drove to the impound lot where Bill ran a full bead on the visible parts of the impounded Chevy. Then he did a strange thing. He pulled a canteen out of the truck and wet the new weld down, after quickly chipping off the slag. I thought he was cooling it down for some reason. But then he pulled a salt shaker out of his pocket and sprinkled salt along the steaming bead.

"What the hell, Bill?" I queried.

"That'll rust in 2 hours. No one will ever notice with all the other rust on this thing and when they finally do - you'll be long gone Smitty."

They dropped me back at Pollution Homes and I went back to sleep, comforted in the knowledge that I could put my car on that ship to San Diego - even if you could see through the spot welds in the back. The sun was just clearing the ridge in the east as I drifted off. My Chevy was seaworthy. To this day I wonder what the KPD thought when they finally discovered that car. Or what the owner thought when he came to redeem it.

In 1961 I re-enlisted and applied for Officer Candidate School (OCS). I took the college equivalency exam and passed, making the list. By now, I knew the drill. I knew that few enlisted ranks were selected for OCS, but those who came from aviation were guaranteed flight training upon graduation. I had already passed a flight physical and AFQT test for aviation aptitude. That is what I really wanted - to fly. Pilots didn't scrape, chip, paint, swab or get stomped by elk.

I waited impatiently and finally received my orders for OCS, only to be asked at the last minute if I would give up my berth to someone else who would be too old by the next class. I was assured that I would go to the following class. I agreed and let the guy take my place and began the impatient wait all over again.

During this wait the Coast Guard changed the rating system and initiated an AT rate designating Aviation. I was an AL rate at the time. Because I knew my chances of even getting into OCS, not to mention becoming a pilot, were slim to none if I remained an AL, I scrambled to get reclassified. In my class of one-hundred and fifty, only fifty were from the enlisted ranks and all but twenty of those were out of aviation. I had to get myself reclassified as AT2 (Aviation Electronics Man 2nd Class), if I wanted any hope of going to OCS and flight training. While I waited for reclassification, I was dropped from the list and had to start all over again at the bottom.

Finally four years after submitting my application to OCS, I was accepted and on my way to Yorktown, Virginia. I considered the appointment a high compliment. I was stoked and committed.

Upon arrival at OCS, I was assigned a dormitory-style room with two of everything in it and a roommate. His name was David Barnett Simpson. He was from Manteo, North Carolina - the Outer Banks. Places like Kitty Hawk, Nags Head and Stumpy Point surrounded his hometown. Simpson was the product of a completely different environment and society than I. His speech was influenced by the Ocracoke dialect of that area and I could barely understand him the first few days. It took me quite a while to determine exactly what "Hioye Tiode" meant. He was the rustic Outer Banks Man, and I the San Diego jock. Dave didn't own a pair of shoes until his high school graduation.

We were polar opposites. I had never before seen anything like Dave Simpson and at first I wanted to count his toes.

The ranks of the Coast Guard are and have been, traditionally since its founding, filled and well served by generations of Outer Banks Men. Dave Simpson was such a man and from such a background.

OCS itself wasn't really that tough, but the instructors were and they drove us to our limits. The academic part was not very difficult, nor was the military curriculum. Especially for those of us with prior military service. But for those college graduates without prior military service it was hard and we enlisted had a leg up on them in that respect. Hell, they didn't even know how to drill. Because I had eight years of prior service, I was made a platoon leader the first week - 3rd Platoon. As Platoon leader, I lead the men at drill in "Full Monte" including sword. During a routine drill exercise I drew my sword in proper military fashion, only to cut my nose. Thereafter I was required to drill with a wooden sword.

Errol Flynn I was not and my only objective at OCS was to graduate, sword craft be damned. Graduation guaranteed flight training. I didn't know that my class ranking in OCS would follow me around for the rest of my career. It would become my Seniority Ranking forever and from these rankings, promotion was determined.

As it turned out Dave Simpson was lacking in some areas like navigation and communications where I excelled. I lacked in areas in which he was proficient, so we helped each other through the grueling seventeen weeks.

We were allowed liberty every Saturday morning after inspection until Sunday at lights out. Such privileges had to be earned. Liberty was issued on a demerit system that was tallied every Saturday morning at the conclusion of room inspection. Accumulate six or more demerits by then and you weren't going on any liberty.

Eight weeks in, I still had not earned liberty. I just could not make it through a week with less than six demerits. Then it came to pass that I gutted through the week without a single demerit. I had only Saturday morning room inspection to pass and I would be on my way to liberty, at last. After eight Saturday nights at the OCS Club on base, I was ready to sample the entertainments Yorktown had to offer. I wanted to go to Colonial Williamsburg and other places - to eat a burger somewhere and quaff a beer.

Saturday morning inspection found me in charge of the room. We took turns each week and this week I had the duty. We were graded on the condition of the room for which we both could receive demerits and on personal demeanor, for which individual demerits were issued. As we stood in the room waiting our turn at scrutiny, Dave and I could hear doors opening and the occupants calling out the cadence of their report.

We waited at parade rest while the OD, ENS Hobart and a cadet acting as Yeoman Scribe made their way down the corridor of rooms. ENS Hobart had graduated the class previous to mine. Needless to say he was gung-ho and by the book - a very enthusiastic young officer. I stood confident that this week I would get liberty. Everything was in place down to my pencil - all regulation. They were getting closer when Dave reached over and jerked my snap-on tie off and threw it on the floor. Astounded, I returned the gesture and while I pulled at his tie, Dave slid his hand inside my shirt and ripped down through the buttons, popping them off. I did the same to him. He threw my mattress on the floor and I threw his pillow down. He pulled my desk drawer out and emptied the contents on top of my desk, so I emptied his into the wastebasket. Now the room was trashed.

That's when the OD and the Yeoman Scribe entered and we snapped to attention.

"Good morning sir, Room 222 ready for inspection - two men authorized - two men present - Officer Candidate Smith in charge," I barked.

They stared wide-eyed at the squalor we had created in a matter of seconds. The OD told the Yeoman Scribe to enter two demerits for an improper report, two demerits for a messy room and two demerits for improper uniform - bang, six demerits. I wasn't going on any liberty nor was Simpson. The OD told us to report to him post-haste after inspections concluded.

We did. Of course, he wanted to know what transpired in the room. Simpson admitted that he already had six demerits and didn't relish the thought of my liberty without him.

That night I was sick of Dave Simpson, so I went to the OCS Club on base to drown my frustration. This "no liberty" crap was getting old - fast. I drank and tried to have a good time with the other poor unfortunates who shared my gloom.

Sunday morning I awoke with a magnitude ten hangover. My mouth tasted like the bottom of a garbage can and my breath took my breath away. As I rolled over to sit up, I realized that I was only shod, nothing else save a watch adorned my body. That's when I fell off the pedestal table and bounced on the floor of the OCS Club. I had fallen asleep or passed out on the table and they just left me there, unable to wake me at closing. How I became naked, I still have no clue. The place was deserted and dark. It was just dawn.

Standing, I let the room stop spinning before I sought my uniform and skivvies. I found them in a crumpled heap inside the fireplace, They were unburned but stiff with the cheer and penance of Saturday night and smudged with soot. I couldn't put the things on - hell, I didn't want to. Either way, with the clothes on or off, I was out of uniform so it really didn't matter. Just picking up the bundle and getting a whiff made me gag.

I decided to make a dash for my billet which was only a little way down and across a grassy courtyard. I clutched the bundle of soiled clothing to my midsection, affording myself a modicum of decency and made a crouching dash from bush to bush along the path. At the entry door, the loud speaker broadcast the following:

" - will the naked cadet who just ran across the courtyard please report to the OD."

I was busted. But even in my diminished mental state I realized, though I had been seen, they couldn't identify me - they said "the Cadet" not "Cadet Smith." I went into my room, stashed the nasty clothes and settled into my bed while Simpson snored away.

Liberty came the next Saturday with Simpson taking the duty. By then he craved liberty dear enough to ship-shape my gear and shine my shoes early that morning.

OCS was over and I graduated fourteenth out of the ninety nine candidates that eventually finished the course. It was good and I was on my way to flight training.

The next time I saw Captain Owen Siler was in 1965 at the Miami Air Station where I had been transferred as a brand spankin' new ensign. The good Captain was the senior Captain on the base and he was the CO. The air station in Miami was at a place called "Dinner Key" (of all the names for a place). I was assigned to temporary duty there, fresh out of OCS while awaiting flight training at NAS Pensacola. The junior officers at Dinner Key gave me a warm welcome and sent me off to catch the noon meal at the officer's mess before it closed, that first day, upon my arrival.

"What a great bunch of nice guys," I thought. "They were so concerned that I didn't miss lunch," I further ruminated. It was a typical new-meat prank. I just didn't know it yet. LT's Billy Ed Murphy and George Krietmeyer were the main insisters that I not miss lunch.

I became acutely aware of the prank's nature when I entered the officer's mess to find all the station's top brass, senior officers to a man, seated for lunch - at Dinner Key. Captain Siler was in charge of the honors at the table's head. I tried to excuse myself but the good Captain insisted.

"No, no, Smitty - please join us - sit down here next to me," the Captain pleaded.

I had no choice now. To refuse would be rude. I sat and the Captain introduced me around the table, recounting our duty together in Corpus and how I had come up through the enlisted ranks to graduate OCS and welcome to my first duty station as an officer and gentleman.

During the Captain's discourse, a steward served a large tureen of tomato soup and it began its way around the table to me. Soon the soup, all two gallons of it, was in front of me. I was traumatically nervous to be dining with all the senior officers. I served myself tomato soup just barely avoiding a mishap. Passing the tureen to Captain Siler who sat next to me, I turned to answer another officer's question and let go of the tureen, before the Captain got a good grip and while my head was turned.

I felt the tureen leave my grasp. It heeled over and sloshed a good gallon in the Captain's lap.

Thus began my duty at Dinner Key.

I wasn't done embarrassing myself. The tomato soup incident had only been a harbinger of shame to come. Over the month or so I was there, I did little odd jobs. Because I didn't know how to do anything, I couldn't be trusted with anything.

I did have some friends from other stations at Dinner Key. George Kreitmeyer, Billy Ed Murphy and of course Captain Siler, who had written my original recommendation to OCS when I was in Corpus Christi, and that made my stupidity somewhat more bearable - at least to me if not to them. I found, at Dinner Key, a bunch of guys - both officer and enlisted - with whom I had served before. I was back in their company again, as a dangerous know-nothing Ensign.

The base at Dinner Key was right on Miami Bay. It was commanded from a large old mansion on the hill above, which served as the Admin building, O Club and Mess. It over looked the aircraft ramp on the bay. The main parking lot was on the hill above the hangar and that is where I parked one morning. On my walk down to the hangar, Colors sounded over the loud-speaker. I stopped and saluted per standing orders. After all I was an officer now, and I had to set some example.

While I stood at attention saluting the flag, a young Seaman Apprentice walked by me on his way up the hill to the parking lot. I was a little pissed that the guy did not stop and salute.

"Hey buddy," I called out, holding my salute. "You're supposed to stop and salute the flag when that sounds."

The guy just kept walking up the hill. I called out to him again, but still he ignored me. This incensed me. I was an officer now. I would not be ignored by some Seaman Apprentice. Colors ended and I chased up the hill after him.

Finally catching up, I got around front to stop his forward movement and confronted him head on. I noticed he was a little scruffy. His hair was a tad long and he had his hat cocked at a disrespectful angle on the back of his head. This guy was a perfect specimen over which to assert my newly acquired authority.

"Didn't you hear colors sound?" I asked.

"Oh, that doesn't apply to me." he said.

"The hell you say. Don't you know that you are supposed to stop and salute the flag when colors is sounded?"

"Look man. I don't have to do that shit. So buzz off."

"We'll see about that."

I grabbed him by the shirt collar and marched his ass up to the OD's office. I wanted a piece of this guy's butt. Murphy and Kreitmeyer were in the OD's office. I explained that the seaman had failed to salute Colors and had disobeyed a direct order to do so. They all rolled their eyes and snickered. The OD apologized to the guy as he lead him out the door. I raised hell over them usurping my authority as an officer . They snickered some more.

The OD came back in and said, "Smith, that guy's one of the extras for the TV show Flipper. They film it here, at the other end of the base."

They all busted a gut.

IMAGES

Larry Williams and I at Helix H.S. one week before joining the Coast Guard, 1977.

Boot Camp, Alameda, Ca. 1957, 3rd row 2nd from right. What a cultural shock.

USCGC Dione
"Full speed ahead"

My room at Radioman School, Groton Conn. Me, 2nd from right, back row. Chighizola far right, back row.

USCGC Nike, sister ship to Dione. I was Radioman 3rd class.

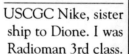

AL School Elizabeth City, N.C. 1959. Me, 3rd from right, back row

Ens. Malcolm Smith NAS Pensacola 1965. I feel I have arrived.

One of my few visits in Capt. Fred Merrit's office in E-City, N.C. without getting chewed out.

C-130 and crew in Hawaii after unloading rent-a-car.

Small boat
harbor Kodiak,
AK, 1971.
Me,in
collateral job
as Capt. of
the Port.

Kodiak 1972. XO CDR. Ed Nelson giving
me a talk on how to succeed in CG

Receiving 1st Air
Medal in CG with
CDR Ron Stenzel
and ADI Ed Nemetz.

Volleyball Team that represented Kodiak in "All Navy" Tournament.

End of a bad day. Front view of CG 1423 after alteration.

Side view of 1423 Homer, Alaska. Lt. Mike Lovett wondering how the hell did that happen?

DEPARTMENT OF TRANSPORTATION
UNITED STATES COAST GUARD

MAILING ADDRESS:
COMMANDER (dl)
17TH COAST GUARD DISTRICT
FPO SEATTLE 98771

CERTIFIED AIR MAIL – RRR
INTRA ALASKA
FOR OFFICIAL USE ONLY

1611
15 August 1972

From: Commander, Seventeenth Coast Guard District
To: LT Malcolm R. SMITH 7647 (550 56 0038) USCG
Via: Commanding Officer, USCG Air Station Kodiak

Subj: Nonpunitive Letter of Admonition

Ref: (a) Report of Investigation to inquire into the circum-
          stances connected with HH-52A CGNR-1423 ground
          accident which occurred at Homer, Alaska on
          19 April 1972
      (b) MCM 1969 (Revised edition) Para. 128c
      (c) CG Personnel Manual (CG-207) Chapter 8 Sec. D

1. Reference (a) is the record of an investigation into the
circumstances concerning a serious ground accident involving
a helicopter of which you were aircraft commander and a parked
HC-130 aircraft. I have given this record my own careful
personal attention and review.

2. Specifically the accident which resulted in severe
damages to the two aircraft and which could easily have
been fatal to both yourself and others seemed to stem from
a conspicuous lapse of sound professional judgment on your
part. I find it difficult to comprehend how or why an
aircraft commander of your experience would attempt a maneuver such as that leading to the accident with such a
cursory evaluation of the close quarter situation that existed
prior to commencement of the attempted maneuver, and with an
apparent disregard for the advance that takes place when an
HH-52A is turned while taxiing. I find it equally difficult
to comprehend why in attempting the maneuver you placed such
complete dependence upon the taxi director for clearance and
safety of the operation, and why you proceeded with the evolution
when you did not have the relative positions of the rotor blade
tips and the horizontal stabilizer in view. You are hereby
administratively admonished to be more careful in the exercise
of your judgment in the future.

3. This letter being nonpunitive is addressed to you as a
corrective measure. It does not become a part of your official
record. You are advised however, that in the future you will
be expected to demonstrate greater attention and care in order
to measure up to the high standards of performance of duty
required of all Coast Guard aircraft commanders and pilots. I
trust that the instructional benefit which you have received
from this experience will cause you to become a more proficient
officer.

FOR OFFICIAL USE ONLY

Official admonishment "to be more careful in the…future."

UNITED STATES COAST GUARD

Certificate of Merit

IN RECOGNITION *of notable services which have*

assisted greatly in furthering the aims and

functions of the Coast Guard

**for his futuristic vision and heroic action which resulted in the
rapid mating of an HH-52A rotor system with an HC-130 empennage thereby
creating the HH52A Cockpit Procedures Trainer.**

This certificate is awarded to

MALCOLM R. SMITH
LIEUTENANT COMMANDER
U.S. COAST GUARD (RETIRED)

Executed this 23rd *day of* January 1991

at U.S. Coast Guard Aviation Training Center, Mobile, AL.

PAUL E. BUSICK, CAPT, U.S. COAST GUARD
Commanding Officer

Certificate of Merit for the same incident
for those of you who have never seen one.

CG 1423 Cockpit as it looks today in Naval Aviation Museum, Pensacola, FL

Standing next to CG 1423 Cockpit in Naval Aviation Museum, Pensacola, FL

Pteros at Roost 1997, Pensacola, FL

PART IV

PART IV

Elizabeth City, North Carolina in the mid to late 1960's, without a doubt, had to be the best aviation unit in the Coast Guard where a fledgling aviator could test his new wings. I arrived as a brand new Lieutenant Junior Grade (LTJG), with Dave Simpson my OCS roommate. Dave and I came from flight training at the Naval Air Station in Pensacola, with only a brief stay at the Miami Air Station, while we waited for our first duty posting as aviators. We arrived in E-city with all the anticipation of the only two kids in a great big candy store.

While E-City was not my first choice of duty stations, it turned out to be the best I could have hoped for. Thank God for answering prayers that are never prayed.

E-City is sixty miles south of Norfolk, Virginia approximately thirty miles inland from the North Carolina Outer Banks, and on the shores of the Pasquotank River. Other than the Coast Guard, farming and fishing are the primary income sources for most inhabitants. E-City actually housed two separate commands on the base - the Air Station and the Aviation Repair and Supply Center (AR&SC). The base was the largest employer in the area and the two commands combined were comprised of active duty Coast Guardsmen and civilian employees, totaling between seven and nine hundred people.

This part of the country is steeped in Coast Guard tradition. It is where the service originated as the "Lighthouse Service," established on the Outer

Banks by James Madison and many descendants of those original Lighthouse Keepers are active Coast Guardsmen in this area yet today. The many Scarboroughs, Grays and Midgetts that serve in the Coast Guard most certainly come from this area. In fact the USCGC Midgett is named after one such family whose members have served for generations.

Because the Air Station was equipped with three distinct and different types of aircraft, serving the numerous and varied missions originating out of E-City, I was provided with an almost limitless opportunity to gain experience as a first tour aviator. In E-City we flew the HU-16 Albatross, more affectionately known as the "Goat." The twin engine amphibian's primary mission was logistic and mid-range SAR flights. The indomitable C-130 Hercules served us well. This four-engine turboprop behemoth handled everything from long-range SAR flights to supply and passenger and equipment transport - among many other duties. The final wrench in our SAR tool chest was the Sikorsky H-52 single engine helicopter. It was our short-range SAR aircraft and did the bulk of our work in that area. With the numerous and varied types of rescue situations we were called upon to perform, and the number of pilots, which at times exceeded fifty, many of us were dual qualified. In other words, some guys flew C-130's and "Goats," while others flew C-130's and H-52 helicopters. In my case it was the latter. There were as many diverse types of missions as their were characters flying them. Looking back, I now realize that was probably a good thing.

Search and Rescue (SAR), is the primary mission of every Coast Guard Air Station and the aviators assigned there. It is what we would all do for no pay - just let us have an aircraft - we'll bring our lunch. The opportunity to save lives is a privilege not many ever experience. The fact that E-City was the only Coast Guard Station on the East Coast with C-130's only increased my opportunities. And they abounded, like Ice Patrol in the North Atlantic, which was a month's deployment flying out of Argentia Newfoundland or Loran Monitoring flights to Europe, the South Pacific, the Far East and the Caribbean. We also used the C-130's to transport the Academy sports teams, the Academy Commandant, The Coast Guard Commandant and a variety of other dignitaries. In fact, there was a special Rosewood compartment that slid into the back of the Hercules for such occasions. We also performed most of our proficiency training in the big aircraft. This stretch of the East Coast that encompassed our operational range is notorious and if not predictable, at least dependable, for its hurricanes and other violent weather. Weather, in combination with major shipping lanes, is the primary recipe for the stew that SAR missions stir in helicopters.

The size of the E-City Air Station was not only calculated in physical layout and scope of missions but also in the number of personnel. There were fifty some pilots and three-hundred and fifty-plus enlisted crewman stationed at E-City. The E-City Coasties are a group from whom I learned one hell of a lot, with whom I laughed, and drank and in whose company I shared some of the most terrifying moments of my life. While there, I served under two different Commanding Officers. At opposite ends of the spectrum in philosophies and approach to getting the job done, both got equal performance from their men. They were Captain Fred Merritt and Captain William Brinkmeyer.

I recall that Commander Brinkmeyer had been promoted to Captain and Air Station CO. Bill Brinkmeyer was a dyed-in-the-wool traditionalist and tradition dictated that when promoted to Captain, he be thrown in the drink by his men. Captain Bill let it be known that he expected his customary dousing as tradition would have it. Duty called and we tossed his ass, albeit gently, into the Pasquotank River. The XO's were Commanders Tom Carter and Dick Wohlgemuth. Commanders Marty Kaiser, Basil Harrington and Oscar Jahnsen served as Operations Officers. Others that had a role or influence on my career were: Ted Murphy, George Krietemeyer, Dave Bosomworth, John V. A. Thompson, Matt Ahearn, Jim Webb, Jim Glasgow, Billy Ed Murphy, Al Pell, Dale Schmidt, Harry Hutchens, Paul Resnick, Dave Ciancaglini, Dick Herr, Bill Ricks, Dick Evans, Preston McMillan, Dave Simpson. Connelly Beachum and CDR Deese Thompson.

The aforementioned group would develop into the future leaders of the Coast Guard and are largely responsible for its advances and development at the end of the twentieth century.

Here are only a few of their stories.

During my tour LT Al Pell was the Air Station Public Works Officer. Some of his duties included the repair, maintenance and servicing of the motor pool, in addition to other duties pertaining to the public works, such as roads, walks and common area facilities.

The largest Coast Guard Station in the world creates some logistical problems by virtue of size alone, hence bicycles were needed to get around efficiently. Pell had been assigned the procurement of new bicycles for the CO, the XO and OPS Commander - the Triumvirate of any Coast Guard installation.

One afternoon at the end of his watch, Pell delivered the bikes to the rack in front of the Admin Building which housed the CO's office. The watch was over, so Al went home for the night without the big three seeing their new bikes.

That night, our Duty Section decided to assist Al by dressing the bikes in full regalia for the CO's arrival in the morning. We sent a driver to the nearest hardware store with cash, contributed by each member of the duty section, to purchase training wheels, handlebar baskets and streamers, reflectors, and bells. The driver returned promptly as instructed. We had a lot of retrofit to perform on the bikes while still conducting our normal course of business. No Search and Rescue calls were received during the course of our watch. We had plenty of time for the retrofit. When Pell returned in the morning, the job was done. The bikes were neatly displayed in the rack.

Pell had not yet seen them and he approached his office, Colors sounded. Ever the good Coastie, he stopped and saluted. That is what you are supposed to do - wherever you are - when Colors sounds. The moment Colors ended, Pell dropped his salute and resumed his walk over to the Operations Hangar and his office. He took two steps in that direction when the air was split by the sound of the CO's voice over the loudspeaker.

"Pell, report to my office."

There was no mistake that it was the voice of Captain Fred Merritt, the Air Station CO. He was the only one who would demand such and everybody knew his voice. We had all heard that loudspeaker call, with our name in prefix.

We could see Pell through the OPS office widow. He was looking right at us. He shrugged his shoulders, as if to inquire what the CO wanted. We did our level best to maintain some composure. We pointed at the bicycles. Pell turned to look in the direction indicated. There, in full view of the CO's office, sat three new bikes with baskets, streamers, reflectors and bells. He turned back toward us with the expression of a man incensed. We couldn't hear him, but we could read his lips. The expletives and vulgarities streamed from his mouth like the Chief of a Black Gang, whose dissatisfaction with his men's work fueled his vitriol.

Over the loudspeaker, the CO demanded again, "Mr. Pell, report to my office - immediately."

Pell proceeded as summoned, still mumbling a stream of curse words and epithets assigned to each of us. Moments later he emerged from the CO's office carrying a crescent wrench, pliers and screwdriver. Now he was further incensed because he desperately wanted to give us the finger, but he couldn't. Not while the CO was watching. His hand came up in a half-hearted attempt to flip us the "bird," but rather than risk further wrath from the Old Man, he just waved us off. It took him most of the morning to remove our upgrades from the new bikes. Pell fumed and cursed the entire time. He did not speak to any of us for days.

We spent a great deal of time in the OPS Center filing flight plans, talking to the OPS Commander about our assignments and the other numerous tasks associated with flying or standing-by for SAR flights.

In the OPS Center, was available the multitude of accoutrements attendant to flight. There were maps and charts, all manner of forms and the little incidentals that flight crews needed or might need. In fact I think we called that stuff "incidentals."

On the window sill, adjacent to the OPS officer's desk and front door, sat a gallon pickle jar of disposable ear plugs. They were of sub-gum extraction that was pliable. When rolled between the index finger and thumb, they would form a tight cylinder. Once placed in the ear, the wad expanded to fit its contours, thus deadening the horrific sounds concommitant to any airfield. As pilots and crews left for their flights, they took some ear plugs. They were pink and could double for Bazooka bubblegum. The same at a quick glance, and only close inspection would reveal just the slightest difference in color.

One morning around seven o'clock, LTJG Dave Simpson and I were sitting around the OPS Center after our duty night, waiting for the day watch to show up so we could turn the damn thing over to them and go home. The OPS officer CDR Marty Kaiser usually arrived first.

"Hey Mal, notice how those earplugs look like Bazooka?" Dave said.

His eyes twinkled with the light of mischief afoot. After all, we were just sitting around OPS waiting, nothing to do, nothing we were supposed to be doing. This is how it always got started.

"Yeah?" I responded with an inquisitive tone, signaling my willingness to participate in good, clean shenanigans.

Dave stood and pulled two pieces of Bazooka out of his pocket. We all carried it. Everybody chewed gum while flying. It was the best way to equalize the pressure changes in the inner ear during flight. Unlike a commercial airlines flight where you clear you ears twice, once ascending and once descending, we had to do it frequently in flight. We rarely stayed at the same altitude for long. Bazooka was the gum of choice.

He unwrapped the two pieces, stepped to the pickle jar and dropped them atop the pile, dead center. The color difference just noticeable enough that you could discern the gum from the plugs.

"Follow my lead," Dave said impishly.

Moments later CDR Kaiser walked in to perfunctory good mornings and overnight reports. Dave, still standing by the pickle jar, reached in and put one of the ear plugs in his mouth (gum actually). It just looked as if he had taken an ear plug. He chewed vociferously and exclaimed.

"Hey, these taste just like Bazooka."

Marty Kaiser looked him over as if considering him for a Psych Exam.

"Try one of these Mal," Dave offered. He reached into the jar. I played along.

"O.K.," I said, holding out my hands, ready to catch. Dave tossed me the Bazooka and I popped it in my mouth. Marty looked at us with abject disbelief.

"You're idiots," Marty said.

"No, really Marty, it tastes just like Bazooka," Dave insisted.

He blew a large bubble. It popped and he sucked it back into his mouth.

"See you can even blow bubbles with it," he chirped through his masticating jaw.

CDR Kaiser reached into the pickle jar, now devoid of real gum. He brought one to his face and sniffed it lightly then popped it into his mouth. He chewed and chewed with a sour look on his face. Dave and I continued to blow and pop bubbles as Marty worked the gum/plug between his molars. I could see his eyes begin to water. I could see his mind begin to grasp that something was wrong - that he could chew 'til hell froze over and it would still taste like an ear plug *or* we were just idiots. I could see in his face that he was struggling with it.

Marty spat the ear plug out like a cowboy expectorates his finished chaw. It hit the wall across the OPS office with an audible thwack. He turned and spat in the wastebasket next to his desk to clear his mouth of the acrid taste.

"You're idiots," he repeated.

Dave and I broke into guffaws. The Commander knew he was had. We weren't idiots - just diligent pranksters.

"Get out of my OPS Center," he ordered, pointing to the door.

He was still spitting in the wastebasket as we passed the OPS Center window with the jar on the sill.

INSPECTION REFLECTIONS

Inspections are a part of military life that everybody hates, everybody whines about, endures and, at least once in their career, fails. I don't know too many guys who have never been cited. If I could remember all the times I was talked to, written up, reprimanded or punished for some infraction during a routine inspection - well it might be some kind of record - not the remembering, but rather the count.

There is a certain inequity and randomness of citation that exists in conducting such inspections. It is akin to the role of a baseball umpire. Only that which the ump sees is subject to his call. He can't just call it if he didn't see it. That certainly is the case with any military inspection. As I recall the ones I didn't pass, I have to chuckle at some of the reasons for my admonishments, especially if the guy right next to me was getting away with something.

It came to pass at Elizabeth City that a Full Dress Iinspection, with swords and dress blues, was scheduled one morning, for 0900 hours. It was to be conducted in one of the hangars. My duty section milled around the outside of it prior to assembly. We looked each other over for any obvious deficiencies in our attire - brass polished, white cap covers and gloves, swords properly hung, etc.

During scrutiny, LT Tom Brahm showed up without white gloves and without navy blue socks - both required elements of the full dress uniform and both unacceptable. We had to get this guy dressed properly and we only had moments to do it or he would be written up and our whole duty section would suffer because of it. There wasn't time or opportunity to fetch socks and gloves. Besides, he obviously didn't possess either. It had been awhile since our last Full Dress.

LCDR Billy Ed Murphy, produced a pair of thin white dress socks.

"Put these on your hands and keep your thumbs tight at your sides," instructed Billy Ed.

"No one will ever notice," he assured Brahm.

Murphy hustled Tom over to the paint locker and rummaged through the stock of paint cans. After some serious rattling and cursing he held up a can of quick dry navy blue spray paint.

"Take your shoes off and pull up your pant legs," he said to Tom.

Tom did so and with the deftness and precision of a subway graffiti tagger, Billy Ed sprayed a pair of navy blue socks on Tom's ankles. He fanned them a few strokes with a shop towel.

"Gentlemen. Voila, navy blue socks," he poked them with his finger.

"They're dry - lets go," chortled Billy Ed. We all formed for inspection.

Right next to me stood Tom Brahm, with socks on his hands and paint on his ankles. The excitement of the moment overwhelmed me and I forgot about the piece of gum in my mouth. The CO and his XO, CDR Tom Carter began to inspect the ranks. When they stood before Tom Brahm we held our breath. The CO and XO moved on to me.

It had worked, they didn't notice the hand socks or the painted socks. As they looked me over a warm glow of satisfaction over came me and the smirk of a man trying to stifle a smile came to my lips. We had fooled them. I gave my gum a chew to prevent a "briar eatin' grin" from consuming my face. The XO stepped in front of the next man. He paused and took a step back to me.

"See me in my office after inspection, Mr. Smith. You know not to chew gum in ranks."

I wanted to scream and point to the hands and feet of LT Brahm. I couldn't believe it. After the inspection concluded, I schlepped over to the XO's office. Upon entry he just pointed over his right shoulder with his thumb, signaling me to enter his office. I stopped to plead my case.

"Sir, the guy next to me had socks on his hands and painted socks on his ankles," I whined.

"Sorry I missed that Mr. Smith, but you got nailed and he didn't," the XO snapped.

He jerked his thumb back over his right shoulder with a scowl. I went in to receive my admonition.

Commander Tom Carter walked in behind me and sat at his desk. As the XO, he was a father figure. He guided and counseled me, admonished and punished when I needed it, and rewarded and praised me when I deserved it. Despite my short comings, Tom always gave good advice and support.

Tom was accustomed to my punitive visits and the next one came at the next Full Dress Inspection.

Once again, we stood in line at attention to be scrutinized by that merciless eyeball of our XO. I stood next to the flight surgeon whose name I can not recall. My other side was flanked by Billy Ed Murphy.

When CDR Carter stood in front of the flight surgeon, he noticed the non-regulation shoes - penny-loafers on the good doctor's feet. Tom nailed the guy. My history of inspection rejections allowed me to take pleasure from another's pain. That, coupled with thoughts of what kind of idiot will wear penny loafers to a Full Dress Inspection, was more than my psyche could handle. I laughed aloud.

Tom stepped in front of me. Busted me for laughing in ranks. Billy Ed Murphy snickered because I was busted. Tom stepped in front of him and he was on report as well.

There is a God of Inspections. He didn't want me to be alone. Tom Carter didn't bust me too hard.

THE GENT-LY BENTLEY

Preston McMillan was a great young pilot and a Lieutenant during my tour at Elizabeth City. He was a GQ sort of guy, who was always neat and pressed - impeccably dressed in the manner of a squared away officer.

At some point and God knows how, Preston acquired a large black Bentley automobile. To go with the GQ thing, I thought. I also thought, "Where in the name of Christ did a Lieutenant in the Coast Guard get a Bentley?" What pay grade was he?

It was a magnificent machine - long, black and shiny and had a big motor. Preston would fuss with it constantly when he was not otherwise occupied with his duties. He washed and shined it. He picked at the chrome with his fingernail. He kept it on base overnight, most of the time. After some weeks of ownership he began to record his gas mileage because the fuel gauge did not work properly.

All this washing, shining, picking and fussing coupled with Preston's incessant daily mileage calculations presented itself to us (the other guys), like a piece of meat hanging on a shed door presents itself to an unchained dog. Pavlov's bell was ringing and we drooled uncontrollably in response. As opportunity presents itself,one must take it. Before us was a young Lieutenant, both consumed and blinded by the love and care he had invested in his machine. He all but begged to be plucked ravenously from the shed door of reality. He and the Bentley - the meat, us - the dog.

We hatched our plot and began to add gas to his car while it sat on base each night. Each night for a week we added a couple of gallons. At the end of the week Preston was astonished at the "incredibly good gas mileage the Bentley was getting."

"Especially considering the monster under its hood," he bragged.

The next week we siphoned a few gallons out each night. Soon he began to whine about the "gas guzzling pig." What could be wrong - check the needle valve settings on the carburetors, check the timing, the valve clearances - what?

The next week we added gas back in. He was maddened. The following week we took some out nightly. Now he was checking the tire pressure, timing the engine, rebuild the carburetors, make sure the emergency brake wasn't dragging - what?

We could have kept this up forever. We were having so much fun at Preston's expense and enjoying ourselves so much that we finally went too far. It was LT Harry Hutchins who brought the Bentley caper to a close. Harry may have been the Coast Guard's greatest scrounger. He could find things. And more importantly he could get them.

One night Harry arrived with a bag under his arm.

"That's for OUR Bentley," he said sarcastically.

We all stood from our chairs in the OPS center to look in the bag. Harry clutched it to his chest and turned away.

"You'll see it later."

Sometime during the watch, Harry snuck out to the Bentley and snuck back into OPS without being seen. Only after he had done that, did he call our attention to the car.

"What do you think?" Harry queried.

On the Bentley's roof sat an authentic London Hack's light. It had the word TAXI emblazoned across its front. It was beautiful. I still wonder where Harry found it. It must have taken some doing.

Preston did not appreciate the gesture. When he returned the next morning, he stood staring at his Bentley for quite some time - not quite sure what was wrong. After a bit of circling and looking he spotted it. He promptly forbade us from touching in his car again. We laughed it up and told him about the "Great Mileage Caper." That night he took his Bentley home and we never saw it on the base again.

None of the participants rode in it thereafter.

J-Vat

John Van Allen Thompson had the notoriety of being the best guy in the Coast Guard to purchase anything from. It was said that his hobby was buying high and selling low. We affectionately called him J-Vat. The moniker fit. It was well known that if you needed something - anything - just get J-Vat interested in it and soon he would purchase the item. Shortly thereafter, he could be persuaded to realize how undesirable the item was or just tire of it and sell it at a loss. J-Vat was the precursor to Wal-Mart and Home Depot. He just did it one item at a time, and on a non-profit basis.

He was also an expert on any subject a person could broach. One particular Friday, J- Vat showed for duty and claimed he was a dog expert - knew everything about it. To prove his expertise, he invited the entire duty section over to his house the next day. He informed us that he would demonstrate his knowledge of dog training. We could all be witness to his abilities, at his place, where he would train his dog to stop chasing cars in our very presence. That the dog had a car chasing problem should have been our first clue. It wasn't. Nor was it J-Vat's. Saturday morning, only Dave Simpson and I showed up, but he was ready for us.

He introduced us to his new six-hundred dollar Boxer puppy. It was a beautiful beast. It either loved or hated cars. It was hard to tell. I thought one might need to know which before you actually tried to train the thing and I said so. Simpson nodded his head in agreement. But J-Vat disagreed - expert and all.

He had removed the hub caps from the passenger-side wheels of his black pickup truck and affixed some cloth ribbons to the lugs of each wheel, then replaced the hubcaps. The ribbons stuck out from the edges of each hubcap like a splayed mop head.

J-Vat informed us that the ribbons would attract the dog to the wheel and when he clamped down on it the resulting spin of the tire would toss him up on the curb, thus and forever breaking him of any automotive proclivities - all at slow speed of course. J-Vat instructed us to hold the dog at curbside while he drove by. We were to let the beast loose when he honked the horn. He backed the truck out of the driveway and made the block while we held the dog.

Presently he came down the street at about five miles per hour. When about twenty feet away he honked the horn and we let the animal loose. It dashed for J-Vat's truck. Barking and nipping at the rotating ribbons, it finally got a bite. The spinning tire quickly wound the dog up and flopped him on the pavement a few times before tossing it under the truck. J-Vat could not see any of this because it all happened at his passenger-side front tire. He continued along confident in his genius.

The dog was run over and killed by the rear tires. Thus and forever broken, literally, of his bad habit.

Not long after the dog's funeral, J-Vat decided that he would like to own an airplane. He figured to beat the high cost of aircraft storage at the local municipal airfield by purchasing a small parcel of land to use as landing strip and storage area for his plane. After purchasing the land, he soon realized that the grass required frequent mowing - for takeoffs and landings. His regular lawn mower was simply not big enough. J-Vat went on the scrounge for a riding mower. He considered a trip to the local Sears as scrounging. Somewhere during his search he found the perfect deal, even for J-Vat. Some retailer was selling lawn tractors for $2,000 - buy one get the second one for $100. J-Vat purchased two riding mowers for $2,100. He was in "good deal hog heaven."

Many of the officers and pilots on base lived in a particular neighborhood that was both nice and roomy. The yards were big with lots of grass. One night I was dining at Billy Ed Murphy's house who lived in that same neighborhood. When we sat down to dinner on the patio, the tranquility of the evening was disturbed by the sound of a small gasoline engine.

"What the hell is that?" I asked Murphy, through a mouthful.

He swallowed. "That's J-Vat on his new lawn tractor. He mows the entire neighborhood now. He's got the other one out at his landing strip," Murphy replied.

"Oh yeah, I heard he got a pretty good deal on those," I remarked. "What kind of plane did he get?"

"He hasn't got the plane yet," Murphy replied. "Just the mower and the strip. I'll bet you could get a pretty good deal on that other mower right about now," Murphy ventured.

Before he managed to get his plane to go with his mower and landing strip, Harry Hutchins talked J-Vat into buying a small sports car. It was a Sprite. He looked a little funny driving the thing because he was so big and it so small. J-Vat was a little vexed at the car's limited performance and complained about it frequently. Harry Hutchins suggested exhaust headers would allow the car to breathe better, thus increasing its horsepower and performance. He waved a car magazine to prove the point. J-Vat had the headers installed at cost of $900. He paid $2,500 for the car. He barely had the car out of the shop when Hutchins pounced again with another auto magazine feature article on chromed engines and associated parts like generators, starters and master cylinders. The article touted the newest trend in aftermarket features and described the increased value that classic car owners could yield from such upgrades. J-Vat went for the bait and started to research the idea immediately.

In short order he determined that the best place to have your classic Sprite engine chromed was in England. At the time the Coast Guard had C-130's flying to England on Loran monitoring flights once every fiscal quarter. The next flight had J-Vat's classic Sprite engine on it. The chrome job cost $1,200.

Once the engine was chromed and reinstalled in the car, Harry Hutchins began to hint that Sprites were not really that desirable any longer and that he did look a bit ridiculous driving it. J-Vat took it to heart and soon the Sprite was advertised on the base bulletin board for $1,600. J-Vat had paid $2,500 for the thing and put $2,100 into it for a grand total of $4,600. Somebody got one hell of a deal on that Sprite.

HAIL FROM THE CHIEFS

One of the finest guys who ever served is my old friend George Krietemeyer. George is probably the single reason the Ancient Order of the Pterodactyl exists and has faithfully served as its President for many years.

Back in the late 60's, George was the assistant engineering officer in E-City and his duties put him in constant rapport with most of the Chiefs. The complement of Chiefs at E-City was significant. They required and had their own Club. George had a good relationship with them and as his buddy those benefits sometimes came to me. The Chiefs were talented and a great group of guys, but of course they viewed us with the same eye that all non-coms see their officers. That perception is at best tolerant and at worst pejorative. Their philosophy in dealing with the officers under their command was simply stated.

"Well, never mind then. We Chiefs will see them through," I overheard one say to another.

It happened that George and I received promotion at the same time. He to Lieutenant Commander and I to Lieutenant. This was significant in and of itself but the thrill was further enhanced by the Chiefs, who got wind of it and invited us to drinks at their Club.

To my knowledge officers did not set foot in the Chiefs Club. Nor was it open to the enlisted ranks or general public. It was the Chiefs. That said, George and I accepted the invitation as privilege and honor. We were told to show up at five o'clock that evening.

I was a little bit late, maybe an hour. Some unforeseen and extended duty had kept me. I pulled into the Chiefs Club parking area to find that, of course, George was already there. His station wagon was parked at the front entry of the Club. I pulled in from his right and parked next to his passenger side. As I got out of my car, I noticed that the driver's door was open and I thought, "that damn George - in such a big as hurry to go drink with the Chiefs, he couldn't even close his car door." I walked around the back end of his car to shut the door before going in - didn't want to disappoint the Chiefs.

As I rounded the back end of George's car I saw that he was lying half-in and half-out of it. His head was on the pavement - hat still in place. My first thought was that he had suffered a stroke or heart attack from the excitement of the Chiefs' invitation. I ran to his side and checked his pulse. When I placed my fingers against his jugular, he rolled his eyes out of the back of his head and cursed me.

He wasn't ill. He was shit-faced. George had arrived and imbibed to his capacity. By the time I arrived he had decided it was time to go home. I found the end result of that decision in the parking lot. I picked George up and he muttered a few good-natured expletives while I put him in my car. He continued his tirade the entire ride home.

When I returned the Chiefs Club it was closed. I never set foot inside for that drink and I was never invited again.

DROP OFF ANYWHERE

Any military service has a range of duty that runs the scale from bad to golden. The overseas Loran monitoring flights that I was lucky enough to participate in were golden. During my tour in E-City, the Coast Guard monitored and maintained every Loran navigational station on the planet. Before the advent of Global Positioning Satellites, Loran Navigational Stations were state of the art. They were manned by Coasties, and Coast Guard air crews regularly checked them for accuracy by flying the Loran signal on all four points of the compass, over the station. It's great duty and a wonderful way to see the world. The stations are located in some very far-off and exotic places. The names of many ring with the promise of adventure, at least to a young Coast Guard flight crew.

One such Loran monitoring tour that I enjoyed was a trip to theFar East, including Midway and Wake Islands, via San Francisco. My good friend Connelly Beacham was along with aircraft commander CDR Basil Harrington. Basil was a fine pilot and a very smart guy. I loved flying with him. We had two nights in San Francisco so we rented two cars for our nine-man crew.

I was the junior pilot on this trip and as such my duties included conducting the pre-flight inspection of the aircraft. I arrived at the aircraft a little early on departure day to perform the pre-flight, only to find the crew, minus Basil, had preceded me by a few minutes. They all stood atop the open ramp at the rear of the aircraft. Behind them I saw a brief metallic glint. I walked up the open ramp to where Connelly Beacham stood dead center of the group. A broad grin consumed his face. Behind the line of seven men, tightly strapped down, was one of the rental cars.

"Connelly, what's the deal on the car?" I asked.

"Oh, this is a great deal Mal! You can turn these rental cars in anywhere," he replied.

I wasn't convinced this was going to be anything like a great deal but I prodded him further.

"That doesn't sound right, Connelly. Are you sure?" I said.

He pulled the rental agreement from his hip pocket and pointed to the appropriate clause.

" It says - return to any of our rental offices," said Connelly.

I read the rental agreement and it stipulated the car could be dropped off at any of the company rental offices.

"How do you know they have an office in Hawaii?" I asked Connelly. Now I had him by the short ones. What? Did he call Hawaii to find out?

"I already called the office here to find out. Yes. They have an office at the airport in Honolulu," he said.

At this time it was common practice to allow personal vehicles on Coast Guard aircraft. If someone was sent to the Bahamas or California on temporary assignment, it was allowable to transport a car or motorcycle for them to use. Hence, I bought in and Basil Harrington had no problem with the use of a car at our next stop - Hawaii. I finished my pre-flight and we took off.

We spent two glorious days in Hawaii before turning in our rental car. Of course, Basil insisted that I handle the whole thing. He wanted nothing to do with it, no matter how innocuous it seemed. Basil was a smart guy.

When I turned the car in, the rental agent looked a bit cross-eyed at the contract, then at the car, then back at the contract. Uncrossing his eyes he looked at me.

"This isn't one of our cars," he said.

"Yes it is," I said. "This is one of your rental contracts isn't it?"

"Yes, but no, I mean it didn't come from this location. Where did you rent this car?" he insisted.

"San Francisco," I replied.

"Well that's not possible. There are not nearly enough miles on it, to have come from San Francisco," he begged to differ.

He thought we drove it over to Hawaii. What a moron.

"Oh, we flew it over in a C-130," I admitted

"You mean this car was stolen from our office in San Francisco?" he demanded.

I could not convince the guy that we didn't steal the car. We had a rental contract. It said drop off anywhere. So here it is. Thanks. See ya.

He called the cops. They arrived in moments and I found my self explaining the whole mess to a Hawaii State Trooper. At first the Trooper wanted to arrest me. But after careful consideration and weighing all the evidence, including the contract, he let us go.

Basil Harrington remained in the aircraft through out the entire debacle. Basil was a very smart man.

The remainder of the trip was routine and uneventful. This may have been the final transport of unofficial vehicles on Coast Guard aircraft. We were not permitted to take a vehicle to Europe on my next Loran flight.

It was a seventeen-day trip. Three pilots had been assigned to the mission. They were myself, LT Howard Lindsey, the AC and LT Dick Evans. Eight air crewmen were also assigned to the flight, including Connelly Beacham, my favorite flight mechanic. I was the junior pilot on this mission so I rotated between seats, to spell the other pilots on the first leg of the trip to Iceland. It is a long flight from Elizabeth City to Reykjavik, Iceland. Approaching the Icelandic coast, we decided to stay the first night in the Capital. Our true destination was eighty miles south of the capital - the Naval base at Keflavik where we would refuel. After twelve hours in flight, another eighty miles seemed unbearable. We would have to drive eighty miles back to Reykjavik from Keflavik, so we unanimously decided to spend the night in Reykjavik. The unmarried members of our air crew were delighted with the prospect of spending quality time in pursuit of "Northern girls (who know how to) keep their boyfriends warm at night."

The airport at Reykjavik is a little different in that the hotel is adjacent to the tarmac. Aircraft can literally taxi right up to the front door of the hotel. We had one night to sample the splendors of this exotic northern capital and we intended to use the opportunity to its fullest. The hotel's proximity to the aircraft made it seem as if we literally stepped from the air into liberty. Just open the hatch and we were not only on liberty, we were at it.

We checked into our respective rooms, showered, changed into our civvies, and everyone went their own way. Occasionally, throughout the course of the evening, I ran into one or another of the crew as I made my way around the various sites and attractions. I spent some time with Connelly that evening and returned to the hotel at a sensible hour. We intended to leave for Keflavik at 8A.M. so I requested a 7A.M. wake-up call. I had imbibed the local beer moderately, and had just flown for twelve hours, so sleep came easily and heavy.

I awoke naturally the next morning without the aid of a call. Rising from bed I walked to the window and drew open the curtains. At first I did not notice the large empty space in front of the hotel. Only gradually as I drank in the morning light with my eyes, did I realize that the C-130 was gone. I spun around and dashed to the nightstand. The clock read 8:30 A.M. I dressed and raced to the hotel front desk.

Yes! They had made a 7 A.M. wake up call to LT Smith in room #123. That was all fine except for the fact that I was in room #132 - they apologized profusely, for when no one answered in room #123 the front desk clerk assumed I had already left and was on board. It was of little comfort. The frigging plane was gone without me.

I called the tower from my room.

"Yes," I was informed, the American Coast Guard C-130 had taken off for Keflavik at 8:30A.M. I called Keflavik to no avail. I could not locate a soul who knew of the C-130's arrival.

I couldn't believe the other pilots had departed without me. Nor had they checked my room to see if I was dead, drunk or missing. I thought it was very unprofessional and then I began to boil. I grabbed my gear from the room and headed to the nearest taxi That's when I got pissed.

A cab to Keflavik cost $80. I hired the cabby, explained the situation and we took off as fast as the old Checker Cab could manage the road. About halfway there the cab blew a tire. A spot of luck would find a tire at a nearby service station - for $100. I paid and we were off again. Finally the base came in sight. As we entered the base I could see the C-130 running up at the end of the runway. I told the cab driver to step on it.

"Get me to that airplane out there," I pointed.

The cabby protested stridently. I reached in my pocket. I pulled out a $100 note and waved it.

"Just get me to that airplane," I insisted.

He floored it for the plane with the blue lights of base security flashing in the rearview mirror. The cabby worked his eyes back and forth between the

C-130 and the flashing blue lights gaining steadily on us. I waved the $100 bill again.

We reached the C-130 before the base security truck caught us. I handed the $100 bill to the cabby, grabbed my bag and dashed for the aircraft. By the time I reached it, the side door was open and the ladder down. I threw my bag inside and climbed aboard, leaving the cabby to explain to base security. No sooner had I stepped aboard did the pilot taxi onto the runway. We were airborne.

Reaching altitude I stepped up on to the flight deck to question Mr. Lindsey and Mr. Evans about why they did not look for me when I didn't show. I sat behind them with my back to the seats. Lindsey made some smart remark that I could not hear because I was not wearing a headset. I asked him to repeat it but I still couldn't hear him so I reached up behind me to remove his headset, so I could hear him more clearly. It did not come right off, so I pulled again from behind and over my shoulder. Still, it stayed fastened to his head. I jerked it one more time sharply to remove it. I was still pissed. The headset and mic came off only after it split Mr. Lindsey's lip and chipped his tooth. Then he was pissed.

He was the same rank as me even though he was the AC, so I had no compunction about giving him "what for?" He shouldn't have left me and I made that clear. He made some further remark about my bullshit story. Our friendship did not blossom over the next few days while flying Loran lines over the Shetland Islands. We had words again. In fact, he ordered me off the flight deck during the entire Shetland Islands flight.

After completing the prescribed navigational checks to the Loran facility on the Shetlands, we headed for London, where we would enjoy a seven-day liberty.

Since I was the only crew member who had flown this particular Loran monitoring route, Mr. Lindsey begrudgingly deferred to me with a query as to were we should land. I explained to the crew (except Mr. Lindsey), that in London there were two choices for us. We could land at Mendenhall which would require a three-hour train, bus and tube ride back to the city or we could try to sneak into Northolt, the Queen's airport. Their jaws dropped at the mention of it. The idea further appealed to them when I explained that all we need do was declare ourselves a code seven, which signified that we had some officer or dignitary of rank on board, and thus allowed special clearance for us to land. The only problem I foresaw was our lack of a dignitary. The senior man on the aircraft was only a Commander who worked the Loran monitoring gear. He wasn't even an aviator.

We landed and taxied up with flashing lights. Upon opening the door we were greeted by a group that was tantamount to an honor guard, all saluting and stiffer than the Vicar's collar. As we debarked, the senior man in the British welcoming party asked where our code seven was. To a man, we pointed with thumbs over our shoulders at the open side-hatch of the aircraft. The Commander stepped onto the tarmac and was hustled off for a debriefing of some kind.

We caught hell immediately, when they realized he was only a Commander and not any kind of a dignitary or ranking officer. Only after a serious ass-chewing by the Queen's Wing Commander were we allowed to stay. The ass-chewing was worth it because we had saved ourselves almost a full day of travel time.

I took the crew to the Ambassador Hotel in Marble Arch. I loved it and knew it from my previous trip. They loved Coasties at the Ambassador. They gave us the key to the bar and we were allowed to drink on an honor system tab. I was in my room resting one afternoon when I received a call from Connelly Beacham. Connelly had gone to the airfield to perform routine maintenance checks on the aircraft.

He sounded distressed and pleaded for me to come out to Northholt. I asked him why. But he only insisted more fervently, refusing to divulge the reason. I hung up the phone and took the tube to Northholt. Connelly had said he was in the Wing Commander's office.

I made my way to the Wing Commander's office after some searching. There, I found Connelly standing at attention under house arrest. An angry RAF Officer, slapping a riding crop against his desk, stood behind him.

"Your man here, had the ill manners as to run up your aircraft engines in the middle of tea," he formally informed me.

We were promptly and summarily kicked out.

"Please take your aircraft to some other facility, immediately," I recall were the exact words. We had to round up the crew, fly to Mendenhall and take the long trip back to London that day.

After London we made several other stops in various countries before we arrived in Sylt, Germany. Sylt is a long narrow island just below the Danish border on the North Sea in the very northern most reaches of Germany. It is a typical location for a Loran station. A great deal of shipping occurs on the waters west of there and a ferry connects the island with Copenhagen, Denmark. Sylt boasted a seven-thousand foot runway. During World War II, it was a Luftewaffe base, but in the late 1960's it was one big nudist colony. People traveled from all over Europe to enjoy its beaches and waters. In the winter, the island supported a permanent population of four-thousand hearty souls. In the summer the population increased ten-fold. It was a miserable place to visit, even for a moment, in the winter. But we were there in summer. Naked women were everywhere.

The Coast Guard station there was manned by twenty or so officers and enlisted men. Loran station assignments were for one year. Most of the Loran stations were located in some forsaken part of the globe because that is were they were needed. After a year on some rock crag or storm swept cape most guys were ready for any other duty. They wanted off that station. Sylt however, was a different case.

Even the CO of the station had put in for a re-up tour and was serving his second year. Sylt was hard duty to get. Guys assigned there just didn't want to go home. There were naked people everywhere in the summer - all summer - all naked. I have to conclude somehow the summer tourist season must have been worth the horror of a long winter on the edge of the North Atlantic.

I come to that conclusion because the whole crew spent the entire time holding or placing towels, magazines or wind breakers over our laps. Every time I stood up on the beach, I felt like a junior high school boy who had just discovered his manhood while rising from his desk when called on. We had a fabulous time on Sylt.

Departure day from Sylt found me in the left seat at the end of the runway performing the final checks, when Connelly Beacham came forward and sat in the flight-mech seat between the pilots.

Connelly got my attention. "Be sure you watch the oil pressure on number three, Smitty," he said. His face contorted by an odd tick.

"What are you talking about, Connelly?" I said.

"Just watch number three. It sounded rough when you ran it up," he said

"O.K.," I agreed.

I proceeded with the takeoff and right in the middle of it, the oil pressure on number three dropped to zero. I shut it down and aborted the takeoff. We spent two more days in Sylt while various tests were made to the aircraft. I will always suspect that the oil pressure problem was contrived by someone intimate with the aircraft. Sylt was hard duty to get.

When we arrived back in E-City, Lindsey turned me in for ripping the headset off him. So I filed a counter complaint about him leaving me in Reykjavik. Basil Harrington was the OP's Commander who received both complaints. To his credit, Basil resolved the issues with his usual aplomb. He had to be the coolest OP's Commander I ever served under in my twenty years of Coast Guard duty. Neither Lindsey nor I received an entry in our record over the incidents and both of us walked away without hard feelings - a result achieved only by the way Basil Harrington handled the complaints. Basil Harrington was a very smart man.

ICE PATROL

Due primarily to the sinking of the Titanic, the Coast Guard took charge of Ice Patrol in the shipping lanes of the North Atlantic, originally performed by Cutters. Ice Patrol, in 1968 was the duty of C-130 crews assigned out of E-City. It lasted for a month and then we were relieved by another crew from E-City.

While there, we stayed on the Naval Air Station at Argentia, Newfoundland. We would fly Ice Patrol over the North Atlantic ten to twelve hours a day, for two days. The third day we had off. Usually we just laid around the base main building. It was an eight or ten-story affair with elevators. The basement had a bowling alley and gym, there was an O Club, a mess hall, rec room and lounge, one floor was for visiting pilots (the fourth - ours), there was a store, a floor for single nurses and schoolteachers and the top several floors were for personnel in transit. It was a well appointed facility and we did not need to leave it on days off. During winter, the weather conditions were not conducive to outdoor activities.

I was assigned one such Ice Patrol as the junior pilot. The AC was a LT Commander whom I knew well and liked, and with whom I had flown before. There was one other pilot senior to me on the trip along with most of the usual flight complement.

One night the base held an informal mixer in the O Club and it happened to be after a ten-hour flight, with the next day off. It was winter and we weren't going any where the next day - so why not. The evening was great fun. The O Club was filled with single Navy nurses, school teachers and transit pilots and we all spent the evening drinking and playing darts. The more we drank, the cooler we thought we were and the prettier the nurses got, until closing time when it was just us three pilots left.

We made our way to our rooms. The AC had his own room and bath across the hall from the rooms, adjoined by a bath shared by myself and the other pilot. We all went down for the night. I lay in bed with a light spin, thinking how glad I was not to fly the next day. Just before I drifted off, the door to my room opened.

The patter of bare feet made me think that one of the nurses was paying me a visit. I thought this was great duty and played possum to see what was up. She got in bed with me and curled up in the fetal position, her back to me and began to snore. I thought this a bit indelicate and un-ladylike so I pulled the covers back to see which nurse it was.

To my utter horror it was not a nurse at all, but rather my Aircraft Commander, clothed only in his skivvies. Hell, it didn't matter if he was in his flight suit, this was too weird. He snored like a sailor swaying peacefully in his rack to the rhythm of the sea. I hopped out of bed and stepped across the room. I called his name a couple of times without response. Sliding through the bath that adjoined the other pilot's room, I woke him to witness and assist me. The night was still young and opportunity presented should not be wasted.

We stood in my darkened room and called the AC's name several times. Still no response. Suddenly he rose to the sitting position on the bed, rubbed his eyes and stood. He walked several steps across the room to the closet door and opened it. He stepped inside but we couldn't tell what he was doing with the lights out, until we heard the distinct splatter of a stream hitting the floor - my shoes more correctly. He finished relieving himself and crawled back into my bed.

Now that was it. I yelled the guy's name. Still no response. He was dead to the world. The other pilot and I hauled the AC, still sound asleep on my mattress, to the elevator and sent him down to the lobby. We chortled and giggled for a while waiting for him to come back up, mattress in tow. We waited - nothing. I pushed the call button to bring the elevator back to our floor. When the doors opened the AC was gone and so was the mattress. It was empty.

We rushed back to our rooms and pulled on some pants then took the elevator down to the lobby. The Steward in charge had seen a guy on a mattress come down a little while ago, but he went back up and when the elevator promptly returned, he was gone.

Oh My God, we had misplaced our AC. We rushed around the building looking down every hall on every floor. We could not find him. We knew he was in the building because the Steward said he had gone back up, so we finally went to bed after an exhaustive search. I had to sleep in the AC's room because my mattress was somewhere else with him. I figured he would eventually come back and wake me up.

I woke the next morning to no sign of our AC. I dressed and went to the mess for breakfast. There I overheard several of the nurses from the night before talking about a guy who "was just dragging a mattress down the hall."

I rose from my hangover meal and interrupted them.

"Where was he?" I asked.

"On the nurses' floor, in the TV room," they answered. They didn't know what to do so they just led him into the TV room and settled him down there. I returned to my meal and finished what I could before heading up to the second floor.

There I found my Aircraft Commander soundly sleeping on the mattress to my bed in front of the nurses' lounge TV. I called his name loudly. He sat straight up on the mattress like a marionette jerked by its strings. His one eyed glower pierced my very soul.

To the side of his head, stuck the bed sheet. I can only imagine what adhesive performed that function. He spent the rest of the day resting.

The Air Station at Elizabeth City operated in conjunction with another and separate command called the AR&SC (Aircraft Repair and Supply Center). It was manned by our fellow Coastie,s but a separate command on the same base. AR&SC was assigned the scheduled maintenance for all Coast Guard Aircraft. Whether by flight hours or by the calendar time, every aircraft the Coast Guard owned went to AR&SC. There the aircraft were serviced much like a car gets a regular oil change and lube. Aircraft have a lot more oil to change and many more things to lube.

AR&SC had pilots assigned to the station. They were not duty standing pilots but mostly engineers and rarely flew except to keep their rating or to complete required training. AR&SC had inventory aircraft. Its C-130's and H-16's and H-52's would be sent out to other bases as replacements for out of service aircraft. Those out of service aircraft would come to AR&SC for overhaul. Every plane or helicopter in the Coast Guard went to AR&SC during its service life.

AR&SC had a plethora of aircraft at any given time and pilots were encouraged to log flight hours and test fly them. Hence, a policy of allowing any qualified pilot to check out one of their aircraft for the weekend as a training mission was adopted.

Certain rules were attached. A qualified air crewman had to be on board. The borrower couldn't incur any cost to the Coast Guard, except fuel. The aircraft had to be parked on a military base. You were expected to return the aircraft in the same condition with only the added flight hours. The range of the flight was limited and you could not submit any expenses for reimbursement. It was a very good system for getting flight hours on the aircraft. And it was a good morale builder for the pilots who could get in a training mission while taking a short weekend trip.

One weekend I decided to check out a Sikorsky H-52 for a trip up to Groton where I went to Radio School. I still had friends there and it was a place I enjoyed visiting. I received permission from CDR Deese Thompson, Senior Engineer at AR&SC, and put the word out that I needed a volunteer crewman. One afternoon the phone rang in the OP's office. I answered and it was my good friend Connelly Beacham. Connelly and I had flown Loran monitoring missions to Europe in C-130's and generally spent a lot of time together. He was one of the best mechanics in the Coast Guard at the time.

The next day Connelly and I checked out an H-52 from the AR&SC and headed north up the coast toward Groton. It was great fun flying along the beach, looking at all the watercraft and female sun bathers. A little past the halfway point during the chit chat and banter, I asked Connelly, "When did you get checked out on the H-52?"

He had always been a C-130 flight mechanic and I was glad to see that he had added another aircraft to his repertoire.

"Hell, Mal I'm not checked out on this thing. I just came along for the ride." Connelly stated.

"Jesus, Connelly you're supposed to be checked out on these things before you go flying around in them," I complained.

"Oh! It's O.K. Mal, look we have the manual right here. If any thing goes wrong all we gotta do is read it," Connelly insisted.

I wanted to turn the aircraft around and fly back to the base and AR&SC. I kept flying. In due course we landed at the Coast Guard Lifeboat Station in Fire Island, New York. Connelly and I had a nice lunch in their mess.

After lunch and paying our respects to the Station Crew, we boarded our aircraft. I strapped in and threw the sequence of switches. The engine turned over repeatedly. It would not fire. I tried again. It cranked, but the engine continued to laugh at me in the voice of an old beater car on a winter morning.

"Ah ah ah ah ah ah ah," it groaned.

Each time I turned it over the batteries grew weaker until dead.

"Ah," it croaked and with that all the lights and instruments went out or were dead.

This was exactly why a qualified crewman was supposed to accompany a borrowed aircraft. I knew it - I just knew, I just knew it would be something. Connelly must have read my mind.

"It's O.K. Mal. I found it right here in the service manual - it's the NG 17% switch - it must have burned out," Connelly assured me. "I think I can bypass it. Hang on a minute while I rip and tear."

He proceeded to remove a panel from the overhead and pull out wires.

In due course, he found the right pair, cut them from the offending switch and stripped the ends to bare wire.

" O.K., Mal just crank it - when it reads 17% yell and I'll touch the two wires together - that should let her fire right up," Connelly said confidently.

I cranked it - it was still dead - no batteries. Connelly jumped down to the pad and said he would be right back. True to his word, he came back about fifteen minutes later driving a front end loader with the bucket full of batteries. He robbed the battery out of every vehicle at the Life Boat Station. He also had several pair of jumper cables and another Coastie from the Station. Quickly, he rigged the batteries in the loader bucket to each other with the jumpers and then that whole mess to the H-52's batteries.

"Crank it up Mal," Connelly said as he jumped back in. He grabbed the two wires of the NG 17% switch and stood at the ready to connect on my command. The other Coastie from the station manned the jumpers.

I cranked it up. The engine turned over like it was hooked to the big grid.

"17%," I yelled over the whine of the engine cranking. Connelly touched the two bare wires together. It fired. The Station Coastie unhooked the jumpers from our batteries, closed our panel cover and we were off.

We left the Station Coastie to put the batteries back in all those vehicles.

Connelly and I arrived in Groton to find a large burn mark along the side of the aircraft - from the hot start. The moment I saw that burned streak along the side, I new things were on a downhill slide.

We had a great time in Groton and the next day we made our way to Roanoke, Virginia to pickup LCDR Jim Webb. Jim was stationed with us at E- City and had made arrangements for us to give him a lift on our homeward leg. Roanoke is about two hundred miles west of Norfolk which is on the normal flight path between Groton and E-City. I knew I would need fuel due to the extra mileage so I specifically asked Jim if they had JP4 aviation fuel at Roanoke.

He said, "Of course they do - it's an airport, Mal!"

We dropped into Roanoke, I found Jim while Connelly went in to inquire about fuel. He returned a few minutes later shaking his head.

"No JP4, Mal," declared Connelly.

I wanted to ring Webb's neck - but I hadn't checked on the fuel. I just took his word for it and now we were low on fuel. Things were really starting to slide downhill.

I checked the maps and charts for a shortcut from Roanoke to Norfolk where I knew they had JP4 and lots of it. I saw a way that I could knock off some flight time by making a straight shot from Roanoke.

Connelly and I conducted another hot start at Roanoke and burned more paint off the side of the aircraft.

Shortly after we launched from Roanoke, a huge stormfront moved in from the south and we were forced to fly a circuitous route to the north. This added more mileage. I thought we had it made when I saw Norfolk on the horizon. That's when the fuel warning light came on, indicating only fifteen minutes of fuel remaining. Things were going downhill at a serious clip now. I made Webb get out of the front seat and sit in the back. I was pissed. I didn't want to look at him any longer.

About ten minutes into the fuel warning light we were still not very close to Norfolk and I knew I wasn't going to make it. That's when I saw the Signal gas station - with the big white tank that read "kerosene" on the side. My mind began to whir and spin like a hard drive. Somewhere stored in the very back recesses, I found a bit that said, "helicopters can fly on kerosene."

I asked Connelly. He shrugged, "I don't know," then madly began flipping through the service manual while I set the thing down right behind the gas station. The station owner was surprised but agreed to sell us kerosene.

Connelly found the proper fuel mixture settings for burning kerosene. While I filled the tank with a five-gallon bucket provided by the station owner, Connelly reset the mix.

Pay the guy - give his bucket back (it was important to him) - hot start - burn off some more paint and we were on our way - spectators below aghast.

"Webb!" I said his name aloud like a curse.

"What?" he said from the back.

She ran a little rough but we made it to Norfolk where we added some real fuel and it ran a little better on the way back to E-City. We arrived in E-City without further incident late that Sunday afternoon.

The next day was, of course, Monday - a normal work day and shortly after my arrival, I was summoned to the AR&SC by CDR Deese Thompson.

When I entered the service hangar which also housed CDR Thompson's office, I noticed the H-52 I borrowed was on the hangar deck - I recognized the burn marks. It looked like they were pulling the transmission and I said so to Deese.

"Yeah, that one was full of sand," he replied. Oh God! I cringed. Here it comes.

"Did you fly low over or close to any sand, Smitty?" he inquired.

"I did Sir. I flew along the beach for a little while," I admitted.

"I see," Deese replied. "What about that NG 17% switch in the over-head?" he continued.

"Well sir, Beacham determined that it was defective and bypassed it. It was the only way for us to get the aircraft back - Sir," I explained.

"I see. I notice she picked up a few burn marks on the side there Smitty," he said, pointing.

"Yes, sir, that was a result of the hot start," I replied.

I purposely did not say "starts" because I wasn't sure if he knew about the kerosene. Any question I had was answered when he asked me to step into his office. Once there, I stood in front of his desk and he tossed a copy of the Norfolk Daily News in front of me. On the front page was a picture of me standing on the helicopter with a five-gallon bucket, pouring kerosene into the tank.

"Webb!" I seethed to myself.

"Smitty," Deese said.

"Yes, sir," I replied.

"Long as I am at this command, please don't borrow my aircraft again," he pleaded.

"Yes, sir, I won't," I promised.

PICKLE THE CABLE

LCDR Jim Webb was senior to me in rank and in years served. I was a Lieutenant and he was a LT Commander. When we flew C-130's he was the AC. However when we flew helicopters together, I was senior to Jim despite our ranks and on those occasions, I would be the AC.

Jim and I were dispatched one stormy day because the Captain of a freighter in Delaware Bay had reported taking on water and requested portable pumps be airlifted to him.

We loaded three cans marked "Pump" and launched late that afternoon. It is a two or three hour flight from E-City to Delaware Bay.

Normally, I would have occupied the right seat as AC, but this time I let Webb take that position. I figured a five hundred foot ship and the open expanse of Delaware Bay would allow enough maneuvering room to forgive any inexperience Jim might experience. We arrived on scene just at the gloaming to hover over the pitching and rolling deck of the big ship.

Normally we would make such a drop on the fan tail of a ship and indeed we intended the same this time. But the fantail was covered with a large tarpaulin and only a five-by-ten foot area was open in which to lower the pumps. The wind blew and the seas rolled. It was now a dark and stormy night, just like that. With some difficulty, Jim held the aircraft in position while the aircrew lowered the first two cans to the deck.

We stood off fifty or so yards while the crewman unpacked the pumps. I radioed to inquire if the pumps were working and to find out if they needed the third pump we still had on board.

Seconds later the freighter Captain came on the air to vigorously complain that the last thing they needed was parkas and blankets.

"Hell yes we still need that third pump - if that's what it really is," he said.

The cans had been mislabeled and we had just lowered a sinking ship winter survival gear. Bad. I had the crewman check the other can for weight by rocking it. It was heavy. It contained a pump. He muscled the crate into a personnel basket and hoisted it out the door, then lowered it to the deck. The air crewman operating the hoist was on an open or hot mic so he could communicate to Jim, hands free to operate the hoist. He alone could see what was happening below.

The ship's crew on deck struggled to remove the pump from the personnel basket. The rolling seas and pitching deck only exacerbated the hoist operators already difficult task of coordinating the actions of Jim Webb, the pilot, with the crew below. He let Jim and I know what was happening.

We could hear the hoist operator on the hot mic yelling to the ships crew below.

"Pull it out!" he screamed into the hot mic. His bellicose instructions were intended for the crew. Pull up on the pump is what he should have yelled, as if anyone but us could hear him.

But Webb assumed the intensity of his yell indicated some danger to the aircraft. He thought the crewman meant "pull the aircraft out." In all fairness to Jim, he erred on the side of caution. Webb jerked up on the collective like you would set a Volkswagen hand brake. We rocketed for the Stratosphere at the rate of two thousand feet per minute. That will put your ass down against the seat. While ascending, a strong wind shear shoved us to the starboard and the whole load swung under the port side of the helicopter. Now, I could see.

We still had the basket with the pump inside, but we also had the entire forty-by-sixty foot tarp snagged on the basket. Ropes dangled and waved from the grommet holes around the edges of the tarp.

This represented a serious problem. If the tarp flapped wrong, it could be sucked into a rotor. It didn't matter which one. Either would do.

Every helicopter hoist has an emergency cable release. It is comprised of a short gun barrel loaded with a .45 caliber pistol round. It is attached to the joint of hook and cable. In the event a load is snagged the pilot can fire the .45 round by pushing a button on the collective, severing the cable and saving the aircraft.

I yelled for Jim to "Pickle the Cable." He did and the load and tarp crashed to the fantail deck of the freighter. They had their pump. We no longer had a hoist.

We spent more time onsite than intended, and we had consumed most of the fuel. We flew to a rocket-launching facility that was nearby on the coast. It was closed. We calculated that we could make NAS Norfolk and refuel there. On the approach to Norfolk the fuel warning light came on so we flew in over the Causeway in case we ran out and had to auto-rotate in.

We didn't run out or auto-rotate but it was close and only a matter of fumes. Webb was still flying the aircraft and requested to take it in. I agreed.

He landed a little hard from about ten feet in the air and broke the tail wheel clean off the aircraft. Luckily he saw it or felt it and kept the aircraft at hover before the tail rotor chewed a hole in the tarmac and ate us all for lunch.

The Navy ground crew at Norfolk worked their magic and hot fueled us with a long hose from a truck parked well out of the rotor wash while we hovered just off the tarmac. They performed the operation in much the same way helicopters are refueled at sea on carriers.

Fueled up, we managed to make it safely back to Elizabeth City. As we approached I explained our plight to the tower and the ground crew was waiting next to a gurney with mattresses on it for the tail section of the helicopter to rest on so we could touch down and shut down without any damage.

"Webb!" I declared in a sigh of relief.

"What?" he said.

While in Elizabeth City, I attended pilot meetings each Tuesday morning. E-City, as it was affectionately known, had fifty pilots. That's a lot guys flying around all the time. Pilot Meetings were essential to making it all happen nice and smooth. At all Pilot Meetings the junior officer was responsible for taking and recording the minutes. I was a LTJG then. The two other JG's that were junior even to me were away on some training assignment. That left me holding the bag at one particular meeting.

Captain Fred Merritt called the meeting to order and proceeded with the day's business. The Captain was not a man to mince words and despite his extensive vocabulary, had no compunction toward vulgarity. Goddamn and M——-f——-r were two words he said most - of any words that he used. So this meeting like all the meetings was laced with Goddamns and M——-f——r's among a plethora of other expletives. I sat in the back with my buddies who were senior pilots and guys I looked up to - Billy Ed Murphy, Harry Hutchins and Dale Schmidt. Two minutes into it I decided, like all JG idiots who knew everything because they were pilots, that the meeting was boring. So, I drew a line down the center of my note pad and made a column titled Goddamns and another titled M——-f——r's.

I started making little vertical lines in each column each time Captain Merit said Goddamn or M——-f——r. Soon I had enough in the Goddamn column to strike out four other lines - meaning five. The count grew in each column. The other officers around me noticed what I was doing and began to titter and giggle. Soon the area around me was a buzz. Captain Merritt tried to continue but the distraction was too much.

"Goddamn it, Smith what hell is going on back there?" demanded the Captain.

"Nothing, sir, just taking the minutes of the meeting," feigning innocence.

"Why are all those officers around you laughing, Smith?" he demanded again.

" I don't know, sir," pleading ignorance.

"Let me see those minutes. Bring that up here Smith," ordered the Captain.

"Shit, I'm busted," I thought.

I reasoned that if I came clean, he might find it amusing or a least go easy on me during the inevitable ass-chewing.

So I said, "Well Captain, I was really keeping track of something in your presentation and I think you have set the record, sir."

"Smith, what in the Goddamn hell are you talking about?" he barked. Captain Meritt could bark.

"That's just it sir, the record I mean. I've been keeping count of your Goddamns and M——-f——r's, and well, sir, with that last Goddamn - it puts you at twenty-seven Goddamns and eighteen M——-f——r's. I'm pretty sure that's a record Captain," I explained.

The room erupted in raucous laughter. When the laughter subsided he looked up from his notes right at me. He was not amused.

"In my office when we're done here, Smith," he said. I started taking notes like a M——-f——r.

The meeting adjourned. Once again after some drill, inspection or meeting, I was on my way to admonishment. I entered the Captain's office which was connected to the XO's by a long narrow companion way. The head was in the middle of the two offices. Guys were in the head and in the XO's office when I knocked and entered the Sanctum Sanctorum. Captain Merritt barked for me to enter and stand at attention. I did so right in front of his desk. As I stood rigid, bracing for the inevitable onslaught of derisions punctuated with the odd curse or blaspheme, my peripheral vision looked right down the narrow companion way into the XO's office. Billy Ed Murphy and the gang were sticking their heads past the door jamb, one on top of the other, two and three high on each side. Their tongues protruded and wagged irreverently. They rolled their eyes and shook their heads. All while the old man was chewing me a new one.

The Captain continued his lobotomized drone of conduct unbecoming, seasoned with blue expletives. While he did, I kept flicking my eyeballs to the left and pointing to my left with my right index finger still tucked tightly to the seams of my trousers. I wasn't about to let them get away with this. They were my buddies and they thought they had the better of me. I persisted with my machinations. The CO stopped castigating me long enough to address my seemingly epileptic fits.

"Smith, what in the Goddamn hell is wrong with you boy?" he growled.

He stood from behind his desk and came around to my right and spotted the "door jamb gang" down the companion way. The heads disappeared instantly.

"I see," said the skipper. "I'll see all of you in here when I'm done with Smith," his voice booming down the length of the companion way.

"Gotcha," I mumbled under my breath.

U F -(uH)- OH

Back in the good ole' days of the Coast Guard, there was an officer by the name of Muddy Waters. He was an aviator and contemporary of our Air Station CO, Captain Fred Merritt. Captain Muddy Waters could lay claim to the dubious honor of being the only Coastie to see a UFO. Captain Merritt, longed for that distinction in the company of his old shipmate. He desperately wanted to see one! It may have been one of his many career goals.

So, the good Captain posted a standing order at Elizabeth City, "that upon report of any Unidentified Flying Object along the Eastern Seaboard of the United States, within flying distance of this Air Station, you will immediately notify the Air Station Commander and then contact Smith."

He never called me Mr. Smith or Lt. Smith and damn sure never Malcolm - just and always- SMITH! But, I was his standing order Co-pilot for UFO searches. HOT DAMN, that was a high compliment. After all Captain Merritt's exploits as an aviator were legendary. In fact, any time the Captain flew, I was his Co-pilot. I guess he trusted me.

I took numerous UFO search flights with Captain Merritt. Some were exciting, most were boring. There was no chit chat from or with the Captain when he was flying. He was all business. Smith do this, Smith do that. Always, Smith. One flight remains vivid in my memory. Late one night into my watch, about 2 AM, I received the call.

"Got one Smitty, the ole' man's on his way," teased the OPS officer while hanging up the phone.

"Shit!" I thought to myself. "Just near the end of an otherwise quiet night and the ole' man wants to go flying," I complained under breath.

"What's that Smitty?" said the OPS officer.

"Lets go flying," I lied.

A Sikorsky H-52 helicopter was made ready and soon we were in the air headed south towards Wilmington. Some Marine jets flying CAPS had seen an array of unidentifiable lights while flying over the Holly-Shelton and Angola Swamps, which are just northeast of Wilmington. On the way down Captain Merritt was his usual silent no nonsense self, so there was little conversation. Finally, we saw the swamps ahead, easily discernable as a huge black hole where no light shone, except the ones twinkling way off in the distance - right in the

middle. Those lights were the UFO. We vectored for them. They twinkled without pause or diminishment. They grew larger and brighter as we approached.

The Captain instructed me, "Turn off the Goddamn running
lights, Smith."

I did so. Captain Merritt began a let down pattern from two thousand
feet to five hundred feet as we continued our approach. The lights grew more
distinct. They appeared to form a perimeter pattern of something on the
ground. As we got closer little flashes began to emanate from within the
perimeter of lights. I remember thinking the little flashes resembled electrical
shorts discharging and how they could be coming from a downed aircraft.

Finally over the site with the lights below, Captain Merritt barked,
"Turn on the Goddamn Flood and Hovers, Smith."

I did so. Guys were running around every which way below, the lights
were Coleman lanterns hung in trees around a still. The little flashes were
small arms fire. They thought we were Revenuers. Hell, technically we were.

"Cut the Goddamn lights Smith," commanded Captain Merritt. I did
so. We got the hell out of there. Back at the base we inspected the helicopter
thoroughly and found one bullet hole in the tail section. Those guys were
lousy shots.

COAST GUARD DAY

In the late 1960's the largest Coast Guard Air Station in the world, at Elizabeth City, North Carolina, held the Coast Guard Day Celebration to display its wares and promote itself. A great deal of effort was put into advertising the event that the general public would attend. I was put in charge of organizing it by the Air Station Commander, Captain Fred Merritt. My duties included an array of assignments, from displaying the search and rescue aircraft to admitting the general public and conducting operational drills and flyby's for the spectators, which included the public, the Air Station brass and the 5th Coast Guard District hierarchy.

A variety of small rescue boats lined the docks on the Pasquotank River. Their reflections glistened and shimmered in its fluid but murky waters. Numerous types of aircraft were statically and magnificently displayed on the base ramp. All were available for public inspection in effort to promote the Coast Guard. A powerfully intoxicating display of the Coast Guard's sea and air capabilities greeted the spectators. Children fidgeted at their parents sides at the prospect of looking inside those planes and helicopters. They fussed relentlessly in anticipation of military aircraft flying over head, with precision and power. The Coast Guard brass puffed with pride in the knowledge that the Coast Guard's new technology and image would have a serious impact on the public. It would also help to provide more funds from congressional subcommittees and command a greater respect for the service itself. After all, that was one of the things Coast Guard Day was about.

Finally, the big moment had arrived for the Coast Guard to display one of it's newest pieces of equipment. Such was the mobile communications center. It was self contained, in a sea going shipping container like box. Stout and of steel construction, the mobile com center could hold two communications technicians and an array of state of the art communications gear, such as radios, telemetry and transponder receiving devices that are integral to any of the thousands of search and rescue or disaster related missions undertaken by the Coast Guard each year. This baby was hot and new and expensive. And it was heavy. But even so, it was designed to be airlifted by chopper to any site that could be hovered over. Today, this Coast Guard Day, was it's grand unveiling.

During this ostentatious display of the Coast Guards might and prowess, I would be responsible should anything untoward take place.

I had instructed the new mobile com center be placed dead center on the tarmac and in front of the line of service aircraft. The crowd's attention was called to the unit. As they looked on, the distinct and unmistakable "whop - whop - whop" of a Sikorsky H-52 main rotor grew louder over head. Out of nowhere the chopper appeared. It hovered above the shiny new mobile com center, a cable and hook in tow. Children covered their ears or jerked at their parents hands while pointing up at the hovering contraption. The brass held down their hats. Ground crewmen deftly and adroitly moved in under the hovering craft to make the connection between load and machine and with a thunderous application of collective, the chopper grunted the heavy mobile com center into the air.

In the right seat at the controls, sat an experienced rotary wing pilot of consummate ability. He had been chosen to perform this duty specifically for his familiarity with dead lift load transports. He was to fly the new mobile com center down the tarmac, along the runway and out over the river, stop dead over the water, hover, rotate the aircraft and then bring the load back over the assembled display aircraft, pass by the crowd and then disappear behind the main hanger on the other side of the packed visitors' parking lot. There he would drop the load and return to hover in front of the crowd without it. Thus displaying it's mobility.

The civilian spectators "oohed and ahhed" as the big chopper lifted the mobile com center off the tarmac and began it's run across the river, some one hundred yards away. They applauded as the aircraft moved along with the heavy load hanging dead still underneath. So skilled was the pilot that not the slightest perception of drift or wiggle in the load could be detected by the onlookers.

At the far side of the river, the skilled pilot stopped the air craft so smoothly that the load remained dead center, again without the slightest perception of drift. He rotated the chopper 180 degrees and began his run back to the base as planned.

Whether due to malfunction, miscalculated load capacity, wind shear or pilot error, the load released. The brand spanking new and terribly expensive mobile com center plummeted one hundred feet to the shallow tidal waters of the Pasquotank River below. It hit the surface with all the impact of a bowling ball dropped into a bathtub and sustained the damage of a cereal box caught between. Its top stuck out of the shallow bank side waters. It's sides split at every corner. Brackish tidal water poured inside the compartment. The salt instantly corroded the electrical components and a faint wispy plume of acidic vapors emanated from the open corners.

Undetected by the pilot, the forward movement of his craft had absorbed the release of his load. He continued his appointed run back. Since, Elizabeth City Air Station shared it's runway with commercial aviation operations, the pilot had been assigned a separate military radio channel as not to interfere with commercial aviation radio transmissions during the exhibition. So the commercial tower could not advise him that he had lost his load over the river. Nor did the Coast Guard radio contact him due to the distraction from a multitude of other communications duties attendant to the day's events. Hence, and regrettably the pilot continued his run unabated, back to the base and over the assembled display of service aircraft on the tarmac, completely unaware that all he had was a long cable and a big hook.

I tried to move to the back of the assembly, out of sight of the old man. I stepped back but nobody made a hole. They were all transfixed on the H-52.

The first aircraft in line on the ramp was a C-130. The Sikorsky approached it dead center. The big hook snagged the long line antenna that stretched between the cockpit and the tail of the C-130. It ripped the antenna off from cockpit to tail like a plucked eyebrow. As the pilot continued his run over the line of aircraft, the hook now with about one hundred feet of heavy antenna cable attached to it, made damaging contact with almost every aircraft on display. Scratching and breaking windows and windshields as it went, pinging off the tight metal skins of the aircraft as the civilian crowd roared - they loved it!

I cringed in horror. Captain Merritt glowered at me with utter contempt. What could I do? No one seemed to be able to raise the pilot, and now he gleefully banked the aircraft making the prearranged pass over the crowd, parking lot and back to the hanger. A sigh of relief was almost collectively breathed at the realization that no one was hurt, until the aircraft's hook and cable snagged the chain link fence that separated the parking area from the tarmac. The five foot high fence slipped off its posts like a child unzips a box of Cracker Jacks. Over the parking lot flew the H-52, cable & hook, antenna cable and twenty or so feet of chain link fence. I winced again, as the chain link fence was dragged across the tops and hoods of parked civilian cars - smashing windshields, indelibly scratching paint jobs and ripping radio antennas and windshield wipers from their very sockets.

As the chopper passed over the last car in line, the old man turned to me and barked, "Smith, will someone PLEASE shoot that son of a bitch down?"

PART V

PART V

Assignment back to Kodiak was a dream come true. I relished the thought of returning as an officer and a pilot. If E-City was the best place for a 1st tour aviator, Kodiak had to be the best place for my 2nd tour. To this day I cannot imagine, but there were actually pilots back then who did not want anything to do with Kodiak, Alaska. I welcomed the opportunity - to fly, hunt and fish in virgin wilderness.

With three years of experience, in fixed and rotary wing aircraft, numerous world wide flights to Southeast Asia, and Europe, coupled with ice patrol, I felt I was ready to test my metal flying in Alaska. It surely would do that. Tasks like flying 150 miles out to sea in a Sikorsky single engine H-52 Helicopter without radar, gave new meaning to the phrase, " by the seat of your pants." In Kodiak I became solely a rotary wing pilot. The Sikorsky H-52 was my ride.

Under these conditions the secret to success became a very thin line between the limitations of man, of machine and what had to be accomplished. To hover on the edge you must know where it is. And on that edge with me was my aircrew whom I learned to trust with my very life. In the class room that was Kodiak, there was no time for day-dreaming.

Some of the strongest bonds I ever established were among those Coasties who lived, loved, worked and played in Kodiak. One of my mentors and heroes in Kodiak was, my XO, Ed Nelson, who liked and put up with me for reasons I could never figure out. I am just glad that he did. My entire bag of good officer traits were acquired from Ed. One Christmas he gave me a letter writing course - go figure. Other guys who had an influence on my life in Kodiak were: Mel Hartman, Sandy Beach, Bob Ashworth , Neil Wagstaff, Frank Carman, Dave Andrews, Benny Watkins, Bill Minter, Ron Stenzel, Lee Goforth, All Pell, Bill Hecker, Gerry Zanolli, Del Phillips, and Tom Preston just to name a few.

One of my favorite experiences was my ancillary title as "Captain of the Port". This duty took me off base regularly to mix and work with the local people. I developed many lasting friendships as a result. It is also noteworthy to mention that rarely does a Brown Shoe, (aviator) receive such a distinction. I was a little embarrassed, as a lieutenant commander to be relieved by a Black Shoe ensign named David Kunkel. Dave Kunkel is a rear admiral now and I like to think I left the Port of Kodiak in good enough shape that he could ride that duty to flag rank - you're welcome Dave.

Three years in Kodiak was all the Coast Guard would allow me. Somebody at headquarters must have realized how much fun I was having. So they sent me to St. Petersburg, Florida. Green benches and shuffle board courts were sores for my eyes compared to the view from an H-52 over Kodiak.

After two tours in Coast Guard aviation, whether pilot or aircrew, the chances of being transferred to a station where you didn't know anyone, were slim and none. St. Pete in 1973 was no exception. To my utter delight I found my former OPS Commander Marty Kaiser as XO and my OCS roommate, Dave Simpson. It was in St. Pete that I met the "Perfect Ensign," Terry Stagg. I grew to love Stagg like a little brother, all 6' 5" of him. In the middle of my St. Pete stint, I heard from my old friend Ed Nelson. Ed was now a captain and returning to Kodiak.

I begged, cried and cajoled until Ed relented and got me reassigned to my beloved island.

I almost forgot to mention between Kodiak and St. Pete and Kodiak, I got divorced and remarried.

GOT HIS GOAT

Not long after my arrival in Kodiak, as a lieutenant, I learned that an OCS classmate was the Chief Engineer on Annette Island. His name was Harold Brown but every body called him, " Charlie Brown." He was a great guy and a damn fine engineer. This was well before the Coast Guard moved the station to Sitka.

The Coast Guard had changed flight regulations and pilots were no longer allowed the luxury of being dual qualified on aircraft. You were qualified for one type and that is what you flew. At the time I was flying H-52's. I wanted to see my old friend but knew I couldn't take an H-52 for a pleasure cruise, (especially on a brand new duty station, besides I had already fixed all that with Deese Thompson), and well—. I hitched a ride on a C-130.

I found Charlie in his office and he greeted me warmly. It had been some time since OCS. I had not seen him in seven or eight years We talked about the good old days and how the place hadn't changed all that much since I was on the elk round up back in '61. The Muskeg, and the Elks were still the only places to go. Every body shopped in Ketchican by plane, motor launch, trawler or the ferry.

About ten minutes into our visit the claxon sounded a fire alarm. Charlie and I rushed outside to see what was afoot. Immediately we spotted a roaring fire in the paint locker adjacent to the hanger. On either side of the paint locker were parked a "Goat," and one H-52 helicopter. The seaplane was closer and in immediate danger. But the Helicopter stood parked with a tow bar and mule attached to it's tail wheel.

A heads up grounds crewman ran for the H-52 to unhook the mule from it's tow bar so that he could move the "Goat" out of harms way. Each type aircraft has a specifically engineered tow bar for attachment to it's nose or tail wheel, which ever the case may be. In this case it was the nose wheel on the "Goat" and the tail wheel on the H-52. The experienced mule operator did exactly the right thing in disconnecting his vehicle from the H-52's tow bar, leaving the bar attached to the tail wheel of the Helicopter to save time - he only needed the mule. He raced the engine. It wound tight, with the mule barely moving, to the "Goat" and hooked on to it's already attached tow bar. He worked quickly.

While the operator was hooking up to the nose wheel tow bar on the "Goat" to his mule, Charlie barreled past me for the H-52 Sikorsky helicopter. He wore no gloves, flight suit nor helmet and head set. Dressed only in his service khakis he intended to move the helicopter out of harms way while a fire crew dealt with the paint locker and the "Goat" was tugged to a safe distance.

He had the engine fired and the rotor engaged before I could say - boo! It was quick thinking and quick action on Charlie's part and at the very least saved the helicopter a good searing, but it almost destroyed the "Goat."

I thought he saw the guy disconnect his mule from the tow bar. but he lifted off anyway - tow bar dangling straight down from the ass end of that H-52. It looked like a bumble bee hovering in for the sting.

Until the tow bar hit the windshield of the "Goat," then it looked like what it really was; a helicopter pilot with a serious problem to which he was clueless. The tow bar continued it's maniacal hop down the length of her back, taking the antenna and just missing the tail section. Men on the ground were running around like piss ants out of a stomped on hill.

Charlie wasn't wearing any com gear. No one could raise him and he could not see the tow bar hanging at ninety degrees. Finally the jumping, yelling and hand waving caught his attention and he was able to discern the signals. Holding the aircraft in a low hover while someone moved the dangling tow bar to a position away from the tail rotor and off the ground, he was able to safely land.

What a visit that turned into. It was six months before I dared return for fear of - well, any thing. Besides, I heard that Charlie had been ordered to Pensacola for phsyciatric evaluation. When I did return, he sat behind his desk, rising he shook my hand.

"Hello Smitty, are you sane? I'm certifiable," he bragged and pointed to a framed certificate hanging on his office wall. It attested to and certified his sanity. A little souvenir from the paint locker fire.

MARQUIS OF QUEENSBURY

I was a lot of things during my Coast Guard career other than a swabby and aviator. This time I was the base athletic officer, the AO, in my view, a less than endearing military acronym. AO not withstanding, Captain Phil Hogue, the Air Station CO, convincingly suggested how I might stage a Fight Night boxing smoker, to raise money for whatever good deed needed doing at the time. I was a good Coastie and I could do more than push rudder pedal and pull collective. I could administrate. I could lead. So I agreed and organized the event with my full vigor.

Flyers were printed and distributed. Prizes were donated and collected. The venue was secured. Contestants were signed up on a challenge basis. If challenged the gentlemanly response was of course, acceptance. Bouts were limited to three rounds with 16 ounce gloves. The Marquis of Queensbury rules applied at all times. Soon the schedule filled with bouts and the evenings card was complete. The Smoker was a sellout.

On Thursday afternoon before the event, I reveled in the glow of a task well done. The base mail arrived while I sat at my desk, feet up basking in the light of utter success. A letter was addressed to me from a galley cook I did not know, issuing me a challenge. The Navy and the Marines still had a big presence on Kodiak at the time and the success of Fight Night was due largely to their numbers. The Navy operated the base and the galley was part of it, so it was staffed by swabbies.

I wrestled with the prospect all that night. So the next morning,, Fight Night day, I went to the galley to meet my opponent. I asked around at the galley and soon the guy was standing in front of me. He was a little guy, maybe thirty five pounds lighter than me and a head shorter. I didn't think he looked so tough, but could not place him and really didn't know why he had challenged me. So I asked him. He had no particular reason - no he didn't know me - some one just suggested he do it.

I broached the subject of our weight difference and my obvious reach advantage - did he really want to do this? Yes! He thought it would be all right. So the fight was scheduled as the final bout on the card.

The evening went well and I gave little thought to my own bout. My numerous school and bar fights gave me a false sense of confidence and my weight advantage only bolstered it. I could handle myself. I had knocked out plenty of guys.

Finally the ring announcer called the bout. We entered the ring, donned the enormous sixteen ounce gloves, received our instructions, (Marquis of Queensbury) shook hands and returned to our corners to await the bell. When it rang and that little cook danced out of his corner with his dukes up, I knew I was in trouble. I lumbered to the center of the ring, guard up in a crouch, waiting for my opportunity to administer one good clout - that's all it would take. As I waited for an opening, he peppered me relentlessly. He was too fast. There was no way to block his blows. The jabs and hooks found their mark most times and if I did manage to block his blow, the force of it only sent my own glove crashing into my face.

It would have been far less embarrassing had he mercifully knocked me out in the first thirty seconds. But he didn't. And although I had participated in my share of brawls and scuffles, I knew nothing of the pugilistic arts nor the Marquis of Queensbury.

For three rounds all I could do was, "stand there like a jackass in the rain and take it."

Thankfully the final bell rang and the fight was over. I lost of course, and took a severe pummeling in the process. Everyone thought Fight Night had been a great success and could not wait for the next one.

Later I discovered that the little cook had been the Pacific Fleet Middle Weight Champion several years before. I never discovered who suggested he issue the challenge.

THE AO

I was the base Athletic Officer much of the time while stationed on
Kodiak. I was a former California jock and suited to the task. It was good
duty. Because Kodiak was part of the 17th Naval District it could participate
in all manner of Navy sponsored tournaments and championships. It was easy
to qualify for such tournaments as Kodiak and Adak were the only stations in
the district. The events ran the gamut from bowling to volleyball and we
fielded teams in just about every one. The Navy paid for all the travel and
accommodations. I took a lot of grief from my buddies over playing badminton, but it was just a great opportunity to get out of Kodiak in the winter.
While they were flying SAR in the ice and snow, I was playing badminton in
California or bowling in Las Vegas.

Bowling was always an easy team to make. Usually the top six guys
made the base team and we all enjoyed a free trip to Las Vegas for the yearly
tournament. One year I did not make the team but went along as the bowling
coach, like they needed a coach. Maybe they did because on that particular
trip, they all forgot their bowling balls and shoes. The team had to participate
with house balls and shoes. On the same trip to Las Vegas for a bowling tournament, we had waited for our late plane in the bar and copped a serious buzz
before we boarded, maybe that's why they all forgot their gear. Some of the
guys were joking around as the plane took off and one thing led to another -
well, some one, (I think it was Al Pell), mentioned high jacking the plane to
Hawaii with a bowling ball. The stewardess (that's what they were called at
the time) did not think it was the least bit amusing. The commercial aircraft
landed in Juneau and the team was hauled off for interrogation by the Alaska
State Police. They let us go once they determined who and what we were.
And that was, Coasties and Idiots.

I played a lot of volleyball on some good teams. But the most memorable
Navy district tournament was a volleyball championship held in Long Beach.

There was such interest in the teams participation that the local newspaper asked me to report in from time to time, which I was happy to do. I
reported back that we had won the blocking trophy. Which in fact, we did.

All the Navy teams had ringers who played in college and joined the
Navy to play. And play they did. We Coasties were stout and quick. Blocking

was our forte. Now when it came to the actual standing in the tournament I may have been a little misleading - unintentionally. I was telling the reporter on the city desk that we had won our first two games, which was sort of true because they were the first two games we had ever won. But I really meant that we had won the first two games of each match. Matches were comprised of the best two out of three games. We won the first game in each match of a double elimination tournament.

He thought I meant matches and I did not correct him. I just didn't want to disappoint the man.

"Oh yeah and we won some trophies," I exaggerated.

Of course we were out of the tournament and we had only the blocking trophy. When we returned home a fan club of one hundred and fifty people or so greeted us at the plane. You would have thought we were the conquering heroes with all the fans welcoming us home and congratulating us on doing so well. I didn't have the heart to tell them the truth so I showed them all the blocking trophy and told them the other one was too delicate to carry, so we shipped it. That seemed to mollify the crowd.

Later I had to go to the XO and confess. He was my very best friend in the Coast Guard, Commander Ed Nelson. Ed was disappointed but glad that I had fessed up. We colluded and no one ever suspected that the team was out of the tournament almost immediately.

BWANA PELL

Al Pell was a Bridge Grand Master and a very intelligent guy. I always enjoyed our duty together and serving in Kodiak gave us plenty of opportunity to do things in our off time. One of those was hunting. Pell decided that he would like to try deer hunting, but he did not own one thing required to hunt. He didn't even own a rifle.

Willingly, I agreed to take him deer hunting and let him use my 243 Winchester. I showed him the proper operation of the weapon and the swing oversight in the event he wanted to use open sights instead of the scope. I suggested that he test fire it to become accustomed to the recoil. What the hell, Pell and I were buddies, despite the bicycle prank back in E- City. I could take him hunting. Arrangements were made. Jim Boteler and I arrived at 4 A.M on the appointed day to gather Pell. He pleaded not ready and would catch up with us out at Pashagshak Bay where we intended to hunt. Boteler and I left without him and drove the forty miles south to Pashagshak.

It took about an hour to get out there from Pell's house. Once parked we made ready, donning boots and coats. Stuffing lunch, water, binoculars and all the other essentials for the hunt in our packs to kill a little time while waiting for Pell. At first light, Pell was not to be seen. We had a commanding view of the entire road back down the Kalsin River. The road below was empty, not a car on it. For the second time that day, we left without him.

We hunted for about six hours to no avail and returned to the parking spot about noon. As we stowed our rifles and other gear Jim said, "Hey, here comes Pell."

Sure enough we could see his VW waddling up the road below us. We gave him a little grief for being so late.

You won't believe this," he said.

"I was driving up the Kalsin and came upon two huge bucks not 100 yards off the road. So I stopped the car thinking I would beat you guys to it and show up with a monster buck on my roof. I got out and swung the scope over because it was raining so hard. Then I braced on the hood of the car for a shot and squeezed one off. The damn thing recoiled the scope into my eye socket and knocked me out cold. I came to laying in the road, on the rifle, in the rain."

"Al", we said in unison while looking at a large butterfly bandage over his eye.

"I'm not sure how long I lay there. I went back to town, got fixed up and drove right back up here. You guys ready to go? I 'm okay, now."

I think Al probably has the scar on his face to this day.

CAPE SARICHEF

Cape Sarichef Alaska had to be the most god forsaken, Loran Monitoring Station that the Coast Guard owned. It was about as far west as the United States goes. Located on Unimak Island, at the very end of the Alaska Peninsula, it was surrounded by the Bering Sea on one side and the Pacific on the other. There was no road.

In the good old days of Loran, before GPS, Cape Sarichef was staffed with thirty to thirty-five Coasties. The duty lasted a year. They were stuck there for a year - a year! The place was remote. Air was the only way in. The station was re-supplied out of Kodiak every two weeks by C-130's. The island also had a substantial brown bear population.

This configuration of Coast Guard station, remote island, air access only and bears lent Cape Sarichef the distinction of the perfect hunting camp. So it came to pass that myself and four trusted buddies, all Coasties, set up a bear hunting trip to Cape Sarichef. We hitched a ride on the regular C-130 with supplies and intentions to stay until the next re-supply flight. Stations like Sarichef were on strict ration due to the logistics of supply and like most remote outposts, the inmates received only so much of any one thing per day. Especially the good things - like beer. The Sarichef crew were rationed two cans per day - for whatever reasons. My guess would be that the Coast Guard didn't want to encourage too much drinking on a remote post - hell, any post.

We didn't care. We brought eight cases of beer with us and several bottles of hard liquor. There were thirty-five guys on the post and we would be with them for a week. The math represented about six and a half beers and a couple of mixed drinks per man over the course of the week. It really wasn't that much over their normal rations - maybe one beer and a shot. They treated us like royalty.

We hunted our way around the island for ten days. We wandered far a field one day to Scotch Cap where the old Scotch Cap Lighthouse was located. All in the party bagged a bear by the last day. The hunt had been a grand success and our hosts had treated us like dignitaries. On the last night, we decided to thank them with a party funded by the remainder of our liquor and beer cache, which was still considerable. It seems the Sarichef Coasties had planned ahead for such a night and stashed the extra rations we brought, by way of just not consuming them.

The evening started after dinner and all those not on duty joined in the festivities, which consisted of drinking and goofing around. We had a dance contest. Guys wore mops on there heads and aprons while dancing on the pool table. Later in the evening,, well into the advanced stages of fun, we held a pissing contest. All the hunters and many of the Loran guys lined up on the side walk to piss in the snow. The snow allowed an accurate measurement without a tape. I can't remember who won. It wasn't me. Some of us were at an obvious disadvantage.

During the entire affair the Chief Electronics Technician, who was also the Station XO, took pictures of the party. No one gave it a second thought.

Back in Kodiak only a week, I was summoned to the Air Station CO's office. Captain Phil Hogue was the epitome of an old salt. Gruff manner and ubiquitous cigar jutting from his set jaw gave little clue at first glance to the genuinely nice guy behind each. I always liked and respected Captain Hogue. Maybe that is why he liked me.

"Sit down Smitty," Captain Hogue invited. " I don't care what the Admiral says - I will not be told who and who not to court martial," he ended.

"What are you talking about, Sir?"

Captain Hogue tossed an envelope of pictures on the desk.

"I just wanted to get your side of the story," he said.

The pictures were a photographic record of the Sarichef party, complete with Coasties in mop wigs and apron skirts. The line of pissing contestants all smiled broadly for the camera.

He handed me a letter from the Admiral strongly suggesting that because I was the senior officer on station at the time and clearly a participant, I should have prevented such events and consequently should be court martialed for conduct unbecoming ——.

It seems the Chief at Sarichef filed a report on our going home party claiming that homosexual behavior was exhibited. The CO at the Loran station was brought up for disciplinary action and passed over for promotion, eventually leaving the Coast Guard. The complaining Chief who made all the stink was ordered for a psychiatric evaluation and discharged from duty.

"No sir, they just can't tell me who to court martial," said Captain Hogue. I still can't remember who won that pissing contest.

By this time I was a competent, experienced pilot and trusted enough by the brass to accomplish a task without giving cause for worry. Ha! Due to my tenure, I became the special pilot for visiting dignitaries and VIP's, whether military or civilian. With that assignment usually went the double duty of fishing guide.

One such time, I was assigned as pilot to the Secretary of the Interior, Maurice Stans. The secretary was on inspection tour and no doubt had inspected some things but the time came for fishing. Of course and as usual, I was assigned to fly him to the Karluk River, which was noted for it's salmon runs. The secretary was a lovely man and I took time to fit him with a helmet for the flight and made sure he had all the right fishing gear before we boarded and took off. The Karluk was about an hour flight from the base in Kodiak.

My passengers were a crewman, the secretary, his aide and the base commander. I flew the usual $5 tour, pointing out all the sights along the way. The secretary was enjoying himself immensely. I had him in the co-pilot's seat so he could have the best view. Around his neck hung a huge Nikon camera in a flashy leather case with a couple of extra lenses hanging on the strap. He appeared to be a serious photographer and I thought he might like to take some pictures.

I flew up the length of Larson Bay on a vector for the Karluk. As I approached the western coast of the bay, a scene unfolded before us that I had never witnessed in all my time flying, hunting and fishing in the Alaskan wilderness.

On the steep, grass covered and treeless slope, straight out the H-52 Sykorski's windshield, a mother Kodiak bear ran with two cubs close behind. On their tails was the most enormous boar brown bear I have, to this day, ever seen. It had paws the size of serving platters. Normally a mother bear would stand and fight to the death in protection of her cubs. But this boar was so big, I am sure the female saw running as her only option. Perhaps her instincts told her that running might save at least one of her cubs. The boar closed on the rear cub and with one sweep of its massive paw sent it careening through the air up the steep hillside. Stunned at least and more likely dead, the cub could not recover from the horrific blow. The bear pounced, tearing the cub open with it's scimitar like claws. It devoured the viscera with both massive paws firmly on the carcass. This was a National Geographic moment. You could wait forever in the woods and never see this.

The forty-five degree slope allowed me to hold the helicopter so the action was happening right outside the secretary's window - right at eye level. He could have almost stepped out onto the slope next to the bear. I looked over at the secretary who just stared dumbfounded by the scene in front of him. I didn't understand why his camera still hung around his neck.

"Mr. Secretary you should get a shot of this, sir. It's a once in a lifetime picture," I said.

He ignored me. I repeated the suggestion. Still no response. I tapped him on the shoulder and repeated the suggestion. He turned to me with a sheepish look and said, " I don't know how to work this camera."

I was flabbergasted This was a picture that shouldn't be missed

"Well, can you fly this helicopter?" was all that I could think to say. I felt a little embarrassed when he disclosed that it was a borrowed camera, which he had not yet learned to operate. He got it - at least the secretary had a sense of humor. I gave his camera to my crewman and made another pass that we might record the event. He was grateful.

We flew on to Karluk and had a great day of fishing. The secretary never took a picture with his big Nikon - of anything.

Not too long after the secretary's visit, I was assigned the duty again. This time the general in command of the Pacific Theatre of operations arrived on a visit, the whole point of which was to fish but was cloaked in the fog of some top secret exercise called Operation High Heels. Operation High Heels was a once yearly drill for response to a national emergency or attack. The intended purpose was to judge the response of the various commands involved. This year Operation High Heels took place in our section of the country and the general had some involvement in it.

The General wanted to fish while he hid out from his command to see how they handled Operation High Heels. The top Air Force general from Elmendorf , the admiral from the Navy base at Kodiak and the general's aide, a major, went along. In preparation for the day trip to Karluk (my favorite dignitorial fishing hole), I set my aide, a lieutenant, to task outfitting the party - he obtained the correct shoe and coat sizes for the party and requisi-tioned hip waders, rain slickers, rods & reels and one giant tackle box from the Special Services Quartermaster. He also ordered box lunches and soft drinks from the mess chief, that our guests might lunch al fresco on one of the true joys of Coast Guard aviation - the box lunch.

The appointed morning dawned and I loaded them all with the general in the co-pilots seat. We took off for the Karluk via the same $5 scenic tour Secretary Stans had enjoyed earlier in the summer.

It was a strange flight. The general was non responsive to my small talk during the tour. I told him and the others, the story of the Bear and Cub with Secretary Stans aboard. I flew them over the same spot but not a trace of the incident remained, nor did we see a bear the entire flight. All during my dis-course the general remained mute. Questions directed to him were answered by the major. Eventually, I gave up any attempt at conversation. And as we crested the ridge of the Karluk drainage, I found the bears. They were feasting on the bounty of the famed river. That's when the radioman told me that a flash message was coming in.

A flash message is the highest priority signal you can get. I switched in to listen. Sure enough it was a flash message for the general. By now I knew the drill, so I told the major, who told the general, who told the major to let him hear it, who told me, who told the radioman. All this transpiring while I am flying down the river. Operation High Heels had begun. The general's response to the message, which he told to the major, who told it to me, who told it to the radioman, who told it the caller was, " handle it - I'm fishin'."

We landed at the fishing spot and I rigged all the rods and passed them out. All the boots and coats had been tagged with tape baring the user's name. I passed them out to each correspondent user. The last pair, the Generals, were two lefts. My stomach sank into a hollow pit. Great, that's all I need now after the silent treatment - two left boots for the guy. Frantically I searched the air-craft while the others donned their gear. The only other pair were mine - not Special Services issue, but my personal pair. The realization that my waders were the same size the general wore was both a blessing and a torment. I had no choice. I gave my waders to the general. I fished in the dorky looking boots all day long like some pour hick cousin. My feet hurt like hell.

The box lunches were a big hit and we all sat around enjoying the brass' delight at the surprise treats our mess always included. During our sit down the general noticed my boots and frowned as he scrutinized them.

"What in the hell is wrong with your feet?" he said.

These were his first words to me. What the hell did HE mean by that? Nothing was wrong with my feet!

"I'm wearing two left boots, Sir," I replied politely, checking my desire to quip a smart ass remark.

"Why the hell you doin' that?"

Okay, that was enough. It was bad enough wearing the damn things with out taking any grief over it. I stood from my rock seat, sandwich in one hand, the other pointing a finger at the name taped to the hip waders.

"So you don't have to general," I said through a mouthful of the best box lunch I ever tasted. The general did not speak to me again. I had to tell the major when it was time to go. When I returned to base I gave my aide the option of going on report for two weeks or wearing the mismatched hip waders for a day. He choose the hip waders.

Another guiding duty involved a congressman of tenure who was a member of the Appropriations Committee. He paid the base a visit while on a fact finding and inspection tour. Fact is, the congressman found facts about fishing and wanted to inspect those areas. That was the main fact. The visit turned into three days of fish fact finding. We decided the best place to take him was Saltrey Lake at the top of Saltrey Creek above Ugak Bay, a couple hours drive south of Kodiak. We picked Saltrey Lake because it had a lodge on the lake and some cabins. And more importantly, there was an excellent Steelhead run on Saltrey Creek then. Lee Goforth and I were the advance team that went over to set up and stock the camp for our three day visit. Lee and I awaited their arrival the next day by fishing for "Steelies" in the creek.

The party included the congressman, his aide, who was his daughter, a congressional staffer and a Coast Guard liason to congress. The congressman's daughter was an attractive, intelligent woman of wit and good spirit.

The congressman's party stayed in the lodge. Lee and I stayed in the adjoining cabin.

That first day the party arrived in several vehicles. Lee and I greeted them warmly. When introduced to the congressman's daughter I could not help but find something familiar about her. I had the feeling we had met before or something. We had a wonderful time fishing that first day and second morning. The congressman was a great guy and made the duty that much more pleasant.

In the afternoon of the second day, they all became exhausted from landing Steelhead and decided to take a siesta. All, except the lady. She wanted to row out to a small island in the middle of Saltrey Lake. Since the bear population was pronounced from the Salmon and Steelhead runs, someone appropriately armed had to accompany our guests everywhere they went, even to the privy. Hence and regrettably, the duty fell to me. It was a beautiful sunny afternoon. The young lady wanted to sunbathe on the island. We loaded a blanket and some lunch provisions and I rowed her out to the island in Saltrey Lake.

When we arrived she promptly laid out her blanket and removed her boots, jeans and shirt. She lay on the blanket in her undergarments to bask in the Alaskan sun. I stood guard uncomfortably, piddled with the boat and generally tried to look somewhere other than her direction. But, that was difficult because she wanted to chat.

About an hour into her sun bath and what seemed days into my discomfort, I heard the instantly recognizable, whop-whop-whop, of a Sikorsky H-3 helicopter. I shaded my eyes from the sun and saw it coming low across the water from the far end of the lake. It was headed right for us. I told the young lady that she might want to get dressed as I was sure the aircraft would pass right over us. She responded slowly and stood up in her under garments in full view as it approached and passed over.

"I'm so grateful your wife lent me these clothes or I wouldn't have been able to make this little trip," she said sticking a painted toe into a leg of the jeans - my wife's jeans. That's why I thought I recognized her. She was wearing my wife's clothes. It was the garments I knew not the woman. She went on to explain how her luggage had been lost and...

"If Captain Nelson had not been so kind as to locate some outdoor clothing for me, I would have been stuck at the base in my business suit."

Evidently Ed had borrowed some camping duds from my wife who was about the same size. She finished dressing and I rowed her back to the lodge.

Ed was standing at the waters edge, hands on hips with a look of utter disdain chiseled on his face. He thought something untoward had been taking place on the island.

"I want to talk to you the minute you get back to the Air Station, Mal," he ordered.

"Ed, nothing happened out there. I didn't even look at her most of the time. It was her idea," I pleaded.

Ed was vexed that I might have affected the Coast Guard budget messing around with the congressman's daughter. Fact was, the congressman had a great time and he sent Ed a letter of thanks saying so. He also ordered one of my paintings on Bear Bread.

Moose Milk is a concoction made from one part vanilla ice cream and one part Vodka, with a dash of Crème de Mint as seasoning. It is a dangerous mix. The imbiber cannot taste the alcohol and drinks merrily at great gulps like he or she were in a soda shop on a hot summer day of their youth. The results usually involved the actions of people who got drunk very fast and didn't know it yet.

In Kodiak there was a standing traditional New Year's Eve Moose Milk Party. We took turns hosting it. This particular year the party was held at the house of CDR Ron Stenzel. Ron was a great guy and the base OPS Commander at the time. In attendance were most of the officers, one of whom was the base surgeon, a fellow by the name of Hans Windenberg. Hans was another great guy and a very fine doctor. He was from Texas. But like the rest of us attending the party, it was Moose Milk time for him also. As the evening progressed, we quickly fell to the effects of the potent milkshakes.

Well into the celebration, we received a call from base security requesting the doctor's presence at the base hospital to attend to the victim of a motorcycle accident. I still can't figure out what the hell someone was doing on a motorcycle in Kodiak, Alaska on New Year's Eve, but there you have it. Of course they needed a doctor. Anyone taking a motorcycle ride on New Year's Eve is going to need a doctor - medical or psychological.

The good doctor went to his duty at the hospital which was across the street and down the block. He returned an hour or so later while the party was still in full swing, just before midnight.

At the stroke of twelve as the usual sloppy kisses and hugs made their way around the party, the doorbell rang. I was standing near, so I opened it. Beyond on the stoop stood the most rag tag, disheveled looking Coastie I had ever seen. He was wearing a torn and grimy uniform, blood on the knee and big bandage around his head. He looked like a revolutionary era fife and drum corps conscript, sans drum, fife or flag. I invited him in and asked what he wanted. He wanted the doctor.

"They said the doctor was over here."

I told him yes that was right and called for Hans. The young man introduced himself as the doctor's patient from the motorcycle accident. Hans recalled and asked what he could do.

"Well, Doc I think I got a problem with this knee you sewed up.", he said

"How so", said Hans

"I went home to rest, like you said and - well I couldn't get my pants off. I think they're sewed to my knee," he declared.

Hans took a closer look to find indeed the pants and knee epidermis were expertly joined by seamless and uniform stitching.

"Shit," said Hans. He took the kid back to the hospital. We finished the Moose Milk without him.

Another Moose Milk party affected the judgment of Hans well after the world was sound asleep. Hans, his wife and his two dachshunds lived in the half duplex 90 degrees adjacent to me. I was in the habit of seeing Hans late at night walking the two hounds. Moose Milk usually occurred during the deepest despondency of winter in the subarctic. About 1 A.M. after such a night, I heard noise outside and rose to look out the window. The view was hazed by a blustering snow squall. In its' depths I could see Hans. He was clothed only in a hospital gown - not the kind the doctors wear, but the kind they give the patients.

"Don't ask," was all I could think upon viewing his exposure. Thank God for the snow squall. He was standing in the yard calling the dogs back from their nightly sniff and spritz. The dogs were named for epithets. He publicly and openly called them by their epithetic names. If you knew Hans, the names were less than shocking considering he once owned a monkey that would perform obscene acts, but only in the presence of women. It was the hit of one Moose Milk party for sure. The dog's epithetic names were just typical Hans. His gown agape at the fan tail, he stood in the snow squall, yelling for each dog to come, by its epithet. Finally he managed to convince them to obey with a bellicose pronunciation of each dog's name. The sound split the night air. Then, dogs tucked securely under each arm he further cursed them with expletives prefaced to their epithetic names as derision for their disobedience. He turned, dogs in arms, to open the door but it had locked. Snow collected on his bare ass. He cursed the dogs. He banged on the door. When his wife did not respond he ran around banging on the windows, cursing and calling her name. All to no avail. And all taking place in the base housing complex. Everyone in the neighborhood could hear it. Porch lights went on around the complex. I left mine off.

Frustrated by his futile efforts to raise his wife's attention, he marched across the yard to the duplex I shared with Gary Stormo, the base dentist. He came to Stormo's place first by the natural lay of the complex but could not get up the steps to Stormo's side. But, he did manage to find a snow shovel that he beat against the house, while calling Stormo's name. I could hear Stormo tell Hans to bugger off, through the party wall of the duplex. Then Hans beat on my wall. I played dead.

I watched while his image faded off in the distance under the snow speckled light of a street lamp, an epithet under each arm, ass shining through the back of his gown. The next day the base radio station broadcast an APB for a man clad in snow boots and hospital gown, carrying dogs, seen skulking in residential areas at night. The base newspaper ran the same story of the mysterious hospital gown clad, dog carrying night skulker.

BATTLE CRY

I had a twenty foot boat. Many of us had boats. It was part of the lifestyle in Kodiak. Hell, we were in the Coast Guard. Boats and planes and such were our life. So was hunting and fishing. This particular trip involved my good friend and XO at the time, Ed Nelson, along with Sandy Beach and Mel Hartman, both fabulous guys. We took my boat to Raspberry Island which is just off Afongnak Island. We had to trailer the boat over the hill to Antoine Larson Bay, launch it and steam through Whale Pass which has treacherous and tremendous tides, to camp in an old cannery on Raspberry Island. Not to worry, all agreed. We were Coasties and capable of negotiating any waters. Negotiate them we did, but not without scaring ourselves rubber legged.

We hunted and had some limited success, maybe a deer and an elk. I don't think anyone's mind was on the hunting as much as it was on the impending trip back through Whale Pass. The return trip was equally gut wrenching . Once through the bad water we came upon some Hair Seals, which were legal game at the time. We were all permitted for such and since I was piloting the boat Sandy Beach asked to use my .243. The same gun I had once lent to Pell and with which he had cold cocked himself. It was a danger-ous weapon.

I said sure and he locked and loaded. We didn't get any seals. Once docked, I attended to my boat and asked Sandy to unload my .243 and put it in the case. He said sure and I continued to secure the boat. I dropped every-body off and went home to find the duplex empty. My wife and 2 daughters were out. I dropped all my gear and guns in the middle of the living room floor, stripped off my crusty hunting clothes and took a shower.

In fresh underwear only, I sat on the couch to clean my guns and gear before putting it all away. I didn't want the little woman to arrive home to a living room full of nasty camping gear and guns. While I cleaned my regular rifle, I turned on the TV to a movie called, "Battle Cry" with Aldo Ray. I loved that movie and knew it by heart. I watched and cleaned my rifle. I fin-ished the first gun and removed the .243 that Sandy hand borrowed from the case. I was in utter bliss sitting in my underwear, cleaning my guns while watching an Aldo Ray war movie - utter bliss.

Just then, as I had the weapon fully in my grasp, the movie came to the part were the Japs are waiting in ambush for Aldo. I raised the rifle and lined the scope up on the TV. The closeness of the set blurred the image into a gray fuzz, but I could tell it was the TV. I centered the cross hairs up on what was assuredly a Jap.

"I'll save you Aldo," I said as I pulled the trigger.

The deafening report of a high power hunting rifle filled the room. The TV exploded instantly. A big hole appeared in the wall behind it. I heard the round strike something metallic in the wall and it ricocheted out under the carpet ripping a 6 foot gouge in it.

"Shit!" I screamed I thought the damn thing was unloaded."

Famous last words. Sandy said he would unload it.

"Oh Shit!"

The smell of cordite permeated the air and it's smoke swirled in the daylight that shown through the windows.

Moments later the base Marine Security patrol knocked on the door. My next door neighbor, Gary Stormo, had reported the gunshot. I told the MP's that I just fired a wad cutter blank into a bucket of sand while testing my pistol and that I wouldn't do it again. They admonished me not to and left.

Quickly I put the gear and guns away and rearranged the furniture so the couch was over the big bullet rip in the carpet. I put a white sheet over the TV to hide its condition. I felt like some idiot on a TV sitcom trying to hide his mistake from his wife. It was exactly what I was doing. How could she not notice?

When she arrived to see the TV covered in a sheet, she immediately thought I purchased the color TV we had talked about. She thought it was a surprise. It was gonna be a surprise alright, when she lifted that sheet.

"You didn't," she said.

"I did," I replied.

"No! You didn't," she said

"Oh yes! I did!" I insisted.

She reached for the sheet. I reached for the door.

BALL PEEN ZIGLER

Bill Zigler was another guy I flew with in Kodiak. He flew C-130's. Bill was a different kind of fellow. He had a St. Bernard named Gretta, to which he spoke only German. It was Bill's contention that this language barrier would prevent anyone from commanding Gretta or stealing her. He was a different guy, Bill was. He drove a Volkswagen Bug. I always thought it comical to see him driving with that huge dog in the backseat.

One day he showed up for work rather beat up. He had bandages on his face and his arm was in a sling. In addition, he walked with a slight limp. He looked a mess so I asked him what happened.

Bill related the story. He was out at Pashagshak. He was fossil hunting on the beach when he came upon an injured doe. Foxes were waiting in the dunes and eagles were circling over head. Bill couldn't let the creature fall prey to the carrion eaters. He ran off the predators and carried the doe back to his car. He put her in the back seat intent on driving the poor unconscious creature to the vet. A noble act at best and an incredibly stupid one at worst. Only moments were needed to prove the later true.

About half way back to town the doe came to her senses and found herself in the back of a Volkswagen Bug. The thing went nuts in the back seat with Bill behind the wheel. It kicked through all the upholstery and head liner with it's sharp hooves. It kicked out all the rear windows. And when it finally gained it's feet and stood upright in the back seat, it started to bite him around the neck, ears and face. It was all he could due to stop the car.

"What did you do?" I asked.

"I couldn't get the damn thing out of my car," he said. "It was really tearing it up, so I grabbed a ball peen hammer out of the trunk and bludgeoned it."

"Your kidding me," I said.

"No, I'm not. Go look at my car."

I did. He wasn't.

The black bear and goat hunt I took my brother-in-law Tom on was one of my favorites. Tom had never been to Alaska and came up from Florida to hunt and fish the wilderness. We were to meet a Coastie buddy of mine named Johnny Dahl on the second part of our hunt which would be for mountain goats. The first part of the hunt we jumped off from Homer via aircraft to a place called Port Dick- appropriately named. It was a successful hunt and we each bagged a bear over the four days we were out. It was a somewhat adventurous jaunt. Tom and I got caught by the tide and had to spend the night in a tent with no sleeping bags. It rained hard that night and I slept in a tree because we were camped on a bear path.

Tom was very happy with the trip and we returned to Homer for a night's rest at the Heddy Hotel, where we met Johnny Dahl. The next day we flew into Bradley Lake which is a high glacial lake about three thousand feet above sea level. I had hunted there the year before and it had proved to be prime goat territory.

The bush pilot landed on the lake and we walked some distance around the shoreline to the same camp I had used the previous year. The trail to the camp was festooned with salmonberries. Tom ate the salmonberries the entire hike up to camp and kept eating them that first day while we set up camp. I cautioned him about eating too many of them and the laxative effects of such consumption. I reminded him of the bear scat we had encountered on the trail. It was full of those berries.

"Nah! I got a cast iron stomach," he bragged.

We set up a meager camp that day. It was stark, due to our limited ability to tote supplies and equipment, but we did manage a three man tent and small stove with some other utensils. We wanted to get things organized in the event weather moved in. Tom continued to graze on salmonberries. That night we feasted on freeze dried camp food and settled in for the night to rest up for the tough next day's hunt. Mountain goats did not live in easily accessible spots. We would have to climb and climb. A good nights rest would be essential. We retired to our three man tent, Dahl and I at the sides, and Tom between.

In the middle of the night I was awakened by a thrashing of the tent. I thought a bear was trying to get in. I grabbed my rifle and felt around for the flash light. I turned it on to Tom yelling for me not to shoot.

The thrashing was him. He was kneeling in a crouch inside his sleeping bag..

"I think I just shit myself," he moaned. "I don't feel so good."

"Well don't get out of that sleeping bag in here," I insisted.

I made him crawl through the tent flap in his sleeping bag. Once outside I shined the light on him while he stood in it and dropped the bag to the ground. The sight was deplorable. To think that a grown man could cover himself in his own waste like that.

But there Tom stood before me in the Alaskan wilderness, in the dark of night, only his underwear to protect him from the chill. Excrement emanated from every opening in his garments. It oozed out the neck and arm holes of his t-shirt. It dribbled out the leg openings of his underdrawers and over the top of the waistband. It was truly a disgusting sight. Even Tom thought so.

He looked himself over the best he could considering the limited light available, then into his sleeping bag before finally turning his gaze back into the light and me.

"Just shoot me," he said.

Tom went down to the lake to wash off. I held the light on him while he bathed in the frigid glacial waters. I don't know what the water temperature was, but all he could say the whole time was, "Just shoot me, please."

He didn't hunt the next day because he couldn't keep his pants up for more than five minutes. We made him sleep outside the tent for the rest of the hunt, in his sleeping bag - shit side out. He didn't eat another salmonberry while in Alaska - or since, I would venture.

ST. PETE

My tour of Kodiak and my marriage over, I drove to my new assignment in St. Petersburg, Florida with my good friend Ed Nimitz. Ed was later killed in an air crash off St. Petersburg. That trip will always be memorable to me because it was about the last thing I ever did with him.

Now a single guy, I was a little on the sad sack side of life but I made the best of it. I guess because I had done so many different jobs in Kodiak, I was appointed Assistant OPS, in addition to Morale and Recreation Officer. I thought it somewhat ironic to be in a low point of my life by virtue of my recent divorce, and to be appointed Morale Officer.

I had nothing else going on so I took the duty and it came to pass that we had a Morale and Recreation meeting. One of the agenda items was the hiring of lifeguards for the summer swimming pool season. The base had an Olympic-size swimming pool and the Coast Guard hired civilians to fill those seasonal positions. During the meeting it was suggested that we should hire female lifeguards only. We picked a three member screening committee to interview the applicants and I ran a short ad in the local rag to the effect of - "blah, blah, blah, female applicants only."

Quite a few young ladies were delighted with the prospect of spending the summer at the pool on the Coast Guard base, with all those Coasties. Part of the screening and application process were field performance qualifications. All the applicants had to be tested in the pool, for skills attendant to such a position of trust. We got to see the girls in their bathing suits before we hired them.

Of course, this all took place before workplace or gender discrimination became an issue. Today the classified ad alone would have sent me to jail. We hired the prettiest girls and considered the matter over and the staff in place for a summer season of pool side relaxation and parties.

Not too many weeks into the summer pool season I received a call from the Flight Surgeon, Lieutenant Chris Nelson, whom I had known for quite some time and we were on a first name basis. Chris asked if he could talk to me privately and I said sure. He came to my office a few minutes later.

"You got a problem Mal," he stated flatly.

I wasn't sure what he meant. "No. I don't Chris."

"That wasn't a question. It was a statement."

"Oh! What is it?"

"I think we have a communicable disease on the base."

"You mean like the measles?" I puzzled.

"No, not like measles. We have a little outbreak of STD on our hands. I've had 7 guys in with symptoms this week. They all tested positive." he explained.

"What the hell is STD?" I asked.

"Sexually Transmitted Disease."

"Oh, crap," I moaned.

"No! Clapp," he corrected.

"Ok Chris, how the hell is this my problem?"

"All the guys have been dating your lifeguards."

"Oh! Crap," I whined.

"No! Clapp," Chris said.

We had to call the girls in for testing and sure enough 3 of them tested positive. I had to let them go. Then to further invalidate the decision to hire pretty female lifeguards, another incident occurred that had international implications.

The British Naval vessel, *HMS Fox*, pulled into the base for R&R that summer. The Brits, of course, had full use of the facilities including the swimming pool. They seemed to enjoy their visit. About three or four days after they left port, we got a call from the American Consulate in the Bahamas informing us that one of our civilians was in custody at the Naval Station there. It seems that one of our lifeguards had stowed away aboard the British vessel to be with her new British boyfriend.

Man that put the crimp on female lifeguards, big time. And just to ice the cake, someone lodged a complaint about our hiring practices with the state labor board and we got a visit from them as well.

The next summer we encouraged anyone to apply.

Another duty that came under the bailiwick of Morale and Recreation Officer was the monthly Officers Luncheon. These monthly soirees would take place at various locations and sometimes we would have a speaker. We had one at the Epcot Center for example. It happened that the base had a complimentary membership to the St. Pete Yacht Club and I thought it would be a great idea to take advantage of our membership by holding the luncheon there.

Each Officers Luncheon was allotted about three and a half hours to serve the luncheon, listen to the speaker and return to base. At the time this luncheon was to occur, a highly touted motion picture was making it's debut in the St. Pete area. So I made arrangements for us to attend the movie after lunch. A little pleasant change from the usual boring speaker. The guys received this idea with great delight and anticipation. I hadn't told them what the movie was but only that we would walk over to a nearby theater from the Yacht Club.

The movie started at one o'clock and we arrived about 12:50 to a long line stretching down the block from under the marquee. All the officers didn't go but there were enough of us to form a significant section of the line and they included my old buddies Dave Simpson, Terry Stagg, Dick Casey, Mike McCormick and Ron Gretto. Upon sight of the marquee all was revealed. The line of men buzzed with jokes and comments. We saw the movie and returned to base.

The next day the front page of the *St. Pete Times* ran a picture of us standing in line in our summer khakis under the theater marquee.

The caption read, "Coast Guard attends the opening of *Deep Throat* starring Linda Lovelace". I caught serious grief over that picture.

Another Officers' Luncheon that stands of note was a little different as well. We decided to make this one grander and sent out invitations to various commands. I made arrangements to have the affair over at McDill AFB. I booked a speaker of note. Somehow I got the Coast Guard's first astronaut, CDR Bruce Melnick. I knew Bruce from some instrument renewal training we took together in Mobile for a week. Bruce had made several space flights and is a true Coast Guard hero. He was giving a presentation at McDill and it was not too tough convincing him to speak at our luncheon. At the time McDill was the unified command for Delta Force. So there were lots of mucky-mucks on base. We invited the McDill officers to the luncheon as well because Bruce was going to talk about his space flights and give a slide show in conjunction with it. This was heady stuff for us. Bruce Melnick was a highly respected and widely know aviator. Several hundred officers showed up. Many senior officers attended - flag officers from Miami, Coast Guard admirals, the disctrict commander and several Air Force generals.

After the luncheon and Bruce's presentation, the floor was opened to questions. Bruce fielded a number of questions when one guy stood up.

"Commander Melnick, with all your space flight experience you must've had some pretty scary moments. Could you tell us what your most frightening moment in flight has been?" he asked from the back of the room.

Bruce put his hand to his head and scratched a little.

"My scariest moment - I don't know. You would think, that it would have been space flight related. But strangely enough, the most seat grabbin' scared I have ever been, was the time I was Malcolm Smith's co-pilot."

Great guffaws erupted from the bellies of those who knew me. The other two hundred or so officers just stared in bewilderment, not knowing who Malcolm Smith was. That might have been the highest compliment I have ever been paid as an aviator.

Terry Stagg was the best ensign in the Coast Guard and should have never been promoted. Not because he was incompetent, but because he epitomized the rank. His huge frame hid a deceptively soft and malleable personality.

With the obvious exception of the Triumvirate, we called each other by first name or moniker. Despite the Coast Guard's penchant for informality among fellow officers, Terry Stagg called every one sir - even the janitor and the trash man. He was painfully aware of his station. That is what made him the perfect ensign. Later in his career, the Coast Guard, in it's inimitable wisdom, progressively promoted him to the rank of commander, thereby summarily ruining the best ensign the service had ever seen.

Terry had just graduated flight training and was assigned to me - which might not have been in his best interest. But we were stuck with each other. It wasn't nearly as bad for me as it was for Terry. I couldn't get him to call me Mal or Smitty - just sir.

One day we were launched to a shrimp boat in distress some miles to the southwest in the upper reaches of the Gulf of Mexico. It was not the classic dark and stormy night but it was a rough ass day to be airborne over the sea, let alone some boat in trouble upon it. Why would it be any other way? Shrimp boats don't have distress on calm seas and bright sunny days. The helicopter was bucking from the time we left the ground.

About twenty minutes into the flight Stagg started to alternate between shades of green and gray. He was breathing so deeply from his mouth, that I could hear it through his mic. He had flown only a few missions with me and this was truly his first time in the co-pilot seat during rough weather.

"You okay Terry?" I asked.

"I don't feel so good, sir. I think I might throw up."

"Negative. You do not puke in this helicopter, mister. Stagg! Do you copy that?"

"Yes sir, I won't. But I sure do feel bad, sir."

"Stagg if you puke in this cockpit, I'll hover 'til you clean it up with your flight suit."

"No sir. I won't."

A few minutes later I looked over to see how he was doing and he had one of his Gortex flight gloves held to his mouth. The opening was stretched tight against his cheeks with both hands. The fingers and thumb stuck straight out like a cows udder just before milking time. Stagg removed the glove from his face pinching the opening shut with the hand it fit. He sat there with a stupid look on his face, still green, holding a glove full of puke. The aircraft bucked in the wind. The glove of puke shook in Stagg's hand.

"What are you gonna do with that now?" I asked.

"Just hold it, sir."

"No! What if you have to take the controls - who's gonna hold it then - we're all a little busy here Stagg and you ain't taking that back to the air station." I said. "Eject that from this aircraft immediately, mister."

He threw it out the window. Moments later he filled up the other glove. He was useless the rest of the flight and he didn't have any gloves.

PART VI

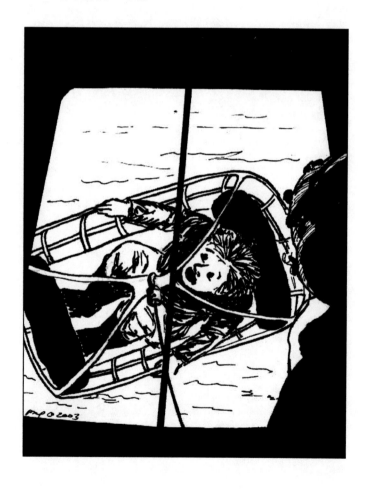

Part VI

I just couldn't have been happier about reassignment to Kodiak, Alaska in 1974 where Captain Ed Nelson was my commanding officer. I was a fourth tour aviator and by this time (my third tour in Kodiak), I knew all the locals well. I had imbibed at Solly's or the Mecca with them and picked enough of their relatives out of the sea, that I could have successfully run for mayor.

To come back to Kodiak with the base totally in control of the Coast Guard, rather than being the Navy's tenant was also a treat. I could see the fruits of my labors from my previous tour when I served on the "Take Over" crew that transitioned the base between services.

This tour I flew the Sikorsky H-3, Pelican. The H-3 was a lot more comfortable and pilot friendly than the old H-52. It had an extra engine and radar. The base also launched the C-130 Hercules for long range patrols, SAR and logistics flights. By this time pilots flew only one type of aircraft and there was always a friendly innocent rivalry between the fixed and rotary wing crews, but it was secondary to the respect each had for the other. However, I am still convinced that the rotary wing guys were better in sports because of the superior hand /eye coordination required to fly their aircraft.

After my third tour in Kodiak I was off to the Old South again, specifically New Orleans, Louisiana, for my grand finale in the service. While flying the Gulf Coast was almost, anticlimactic and "ho-hum", compared to Kodiak, the crew and "krewe" were anything but mundane. A great mix of old shipmates and bright youngsters made up the duty roster down on the bayou. Old mates like Benny Watkins, Chuck Peterson, Dave Kennedy and the perfect ensign (now a lieutenant) Terry Stagg, and the black shoe ensign that replaced me in Kodiak, Dave Kunkel, also now a lieutenant, were joined by some new friends for life, Paul Busick and John Whiddon, all made my last duty station a memorable one.

On July 6th 1977, my twentieth anniversary in the Coast Guard,

Chuck Peterson and myself dumped a Sikorsky H-3 Pelican helicopter off a sixty foot platform at Head of Passes in the Mississippi River delta. I remember getting back to the station in that helo with all the rivets popped out of the belly from hitting the water so hard, still leaking like a sieve and asking God if he were trying to tell me something - 'cause I was listening. The next day I put in for retirement and surprisingly it was accepted.

DARTS

My third tour in Kodiak was a likely candidate for hall of fame duty. My best buddy was the boss and I was a senior pilot, flying in one of the most breathtaking spots on the globe. At least, that's what the brochure says. Flying out of Kodiak was some of the most demanding a pilot could undertake anywhere in the world. Conditions could and would be abominable. Rain, snow, sleet, wind, gales, squalls, fog, clouds, mountains, cliffs, jutting rocks and the dark of night were all normal flying conditions. Nothing ever happened to evoke Coast Guard response on clear sunny days, of which there weren't many. We worked hard and those conditions truly tested and brought out the best in everybody. On the surface the mood was artificially calm and even bon vivant, but underneath it all everybody was tensed for action. Shit happened in Kodiak, on a regular basis. Each man was well experienced in his field, whether it be the type of aircraft he flew in or whether he serviced it. We were all second or third tour aviators

And so as we worked, we played. The base was nothing more and nothing less than a big family and we all played together to relieve the tension at every opportunity. In fact, great effort was expended to produce those opportunities. And so it developed that the games of darts, poker, pool and ping pong became the great panacea of stress for virtually all the aviators stationed there.

Duty nights were some of the most fun times I have ever spent. I almost looked forward to spending every third night on duty. If the night where free of rescues and I wasn't flying, I would be involved in some competition with the other guys. Darts actually became the preferred of those diversions. I think that Coasties and Fireman are probably the best darts and ping pong players you can find. They get a lot of practice while waiting for the claxon.

Everybody had a dart board in their house somewhere, whether basement or garage. We had dart boards on the base and I had one in my office which was located on the second floor mezzanine at the very back end of the hanger. It was well out of harms way and even further from the mainstream of activities in the hanger. It was as far away from Ed's office as I could get and still be in the hangar. It was adjacent to the Ready Room and a door connected the two. Anytime someone had a little spare time they would congregate in my office to play darts among other things. We played darts before work, after work, at lunch and during duty night - whenever there was a lull.

Over the course of my third tour I held numerous jobs at the base other than flying helicopters. I was traffic court judge, base athletic officer, survival equipment officer and assistant OPS. So it was not unusual for someone to be in my office almost all the time and most of the time there were several some-one's. We would conduct business but inevitably a dart game would ensue.

I think, I was the second best darts player in the Coast Guard back then. That was, my claim. There was another guy, named Charlie Hughes, whom I never had the opportunity to play. But, I gave him the benefit of the doubt and laid claim to second based on his reputation. Rumor had him to be the best pool and dart player in the service.

Now some may not agree with my self-awarded ranking. I am referring to Franny (Jim Wright). Franny and I lived in the same four-plex and shared a basement. I am not ashamed to say the amount of time I spent in the game of darts. I consider it time well spent in the development of a cool head and a keen eye. Franny still owes me $35,000 dollars - his losins' over the time we served together in Kodiak. However, this preoccupation with darts went even further. We played any time we could.

But to do so we risked the firey wrath of Ed Nelson. With the ingenuity that is a credit to my Coast Guard training, I minimized the chances of being caught just like I would minimize my risk in flight. I set up a series of mirrors from my office through the adjoining door of the Ready Room and out it's hall door. This afforded a clear and unobstructed view of the entire length of the sec-ond floor hall along which Ed would walk to reach my office. I could see him coming from anywhere in my office. Now, we could play darts with impunity.

At any given time of the day, four or so guys would be playing darts in my office. Of course the desks would be laid out with aircraft manuals and other paper work in the event Ed or the XO did come down the hall. On those occasions the darts would quickly go into a drawer and manuals would be held or leaned over. This little deception had been going on for some time when Ed strolled into my office one day and scared the living crap out of me. On the rare occasion that no one had been in my office, I was deep in paper work and never thought to look at the mirror. Why would I? I was doing what

I should be doing. Ed wasn't going to have a problem with that.

"Ed, what's u?" I said as he looked around my office and into the Ready Room and then into the mirror.

"The coast is clear, play me a game," he said.

I played a game with him and he left.

This became an infrequent but regular event. We did not want Ed to catch us playing darts when he thought we should be doing something else and he did not want his men to catch him in the act, should he ever need to crack down on the darts.

It was a constant dance for me. I never told anyone about the little arrangement with Ed. It just shows what a great CO he was.

Having the Air Station CO as friend was no free lunch. Because Ed and I were close, he rode me like a cowboy on a cantankerous Bronc - tight reign, chunk a mane and sink spur. Rightfully so, I suppose, from his point of view, that no misconception of preferential treatment from our friendship should be perceived by anyone. It got to the point that Ed preferred I didn't put in for things that I was due, during the normal course of my tenure. I mentioned this to him one day in passing while sitting in his office.

"Jeez Ed, I don't know if being your friend is really worth the trouble. I can't even get what's coming to me because of it," I complained.

"I'll give you what's coming to you right now," he said. "You're the new Base Traffic Court Judge, congratulations. Dave Kennedy has it this week. You might want to go watch how he does it because you start next Wednesday and every other Wednesday thereafter."

I was dumbfounded.

I found myself conducting traffic court for the base which included the Coast Guard Station and the Coast Guard Air Station, which Ed commanded. I think Dave Kennedy might have been a little harder on the defendants because my court always seemed to be packed. The court handled all on base traffic and parking violations and infractions of which a plethora abounded. Base Security patrolled just like regular cops and gave violators citations for all manner of traffic offenses. I dealt with them all.

Ed's youngest son, Keith, who was about sixteen at the time, had received a speeding ticket. Ed made special effort to assure I threw the book at him. I think the kid was doing thirty-five in a twenty miles-per-hour zone. Fifteen miles over the limit is a pretty serious offense in any traffic corridor, not to mention the confines of a military installation.

I felt sorry for the kid. Hell, I knew him like a nephew. We hunted and fished together and I had spent a great deal of time with him. I made him sweat a little before I let him off with a deferred sentence and some community service. Ed was satisfied and the kid got the message.

Another memorable proceeding found me presiding over a packed court room with the Coast Guard Base CO's wife as a defendant. The Air Station was a tenant of the Coast Guard Base. Ed ran the Air Station. Captain Parks ran the Coast Guard Base. Mrs. Parks was sitting before me.

When Ed learned she had been cited by Base Security he was livid.

"What kind of a moron gives the Base CO's wife a ticket for going five miles over the limit- let alone even pulls her over?" he fumed.

Nonetheless there she sat, front and center, first case on the courts docket. She was, of course, dressed befitting a lady of her station - suit, hat, gloves and pocketbook. It was all I could do to call the case, but call it I did.

Mrs. Parks was remorseful from the start and the court recognized her as a redeemable member of society, hence deferring sentencing in lieu of a stern admonition to mind the posted speed limits while driving on base.

She thanked the court and so did Captain Parks with a note a few days later.

Captain Siler and I met again in Kodiak sometime during my third tour, from 1972 to 1974. By this time Captain Siler was Admiral Siler, [the] Commandant of the U.S. Coast Guard. He was making an inspection tour of the district and his stop over in Kodiak was a fairly big deal. One night during his tour a no-host dinner was scheduled at the O' Club for all the base officers and their wives, totaling maybe a few hundred people. The highlight of the dinner was to be a few words from the admiral.

The admiral spoke a few words of praise and encouragement, job well done, "Semper Par" and that sort of thing. When he finished his remarks he began to fumble around in his pocket while still at the speakers lectern. Laboriously, he extracted a crumpled sheet of paper and straightened it on the lectern.

"I'll be," he said. "What is this? Oh! Yes, I nearly forgot," he went on. I've been carrying this in my pocket since 1965 on the off chance that I would run into LCDR Malcolm Smith, who I see in attendance. Hope you enjoyed the soup Mr. Smith, this is the cleaning bill for a set of khakis soiled with tomato soup, which I would like to submit to you for reimbursement."

Of course no one in the room had any idea what the commandant was talking about, but I sure did. I could feel the heat from my red ears warming my shoulders.

"Why are you so red?" my wife queried.

"The tomato soup is very hot," was my only reply.

STAGG LUNCHES.

Right toward the end of my career in the Coast Guard I was a senior LDCR on the CDR's list, which had just come out. I was stationed in New Orleans. I new my chance at CDR was slim, as I was getting out soon. They sure in the hell weren't going to make me a CDR before retiring so they could send me a bigger pension check.

Terry Stagg was stationed with me again and he had been ruined as the perfect ensign by the process of promotion. He was a lieutenant this time - a "know it all" lieutenant.

One day Lieutenant Dave Kunkel and myself were assigned to fly the 8th Coast Guard District Commander (the admiral) up to Baton Rouge for a lengthy meeting with the Governor. Because we would land the helicopter on the playing field at LSU we had to stay with the aircraft most of the day until the admiral finished his business. To aid our comfort, box lunches were provided for Dave, myself and two crewmen. A fifth was kept in the cockpit in case the admiral didn't get the chance to eat or just wanted a bite on the way home.

Late in the day, after holding out as long as we could until the boredom of watching some cheerleaders practice overcame us, we opened the box lunches to break it's grip. I always enjoyed a good box lunch and the ones in New Orleans were always a treat - especially if the admiral was on board.

I was hungry. We had spent a long boring wait with no end in sight. I tore open the box. Inside, atop the lunch, was the most vile note I had ever seen in print. The writer alluded to the mayonnaise on the sandwiches as some bodily discharge and assured the diner that because of the color of the brownie he would never discern or detect the substance smeared on it.

I munched a bite of the sandwich and handed the note to Kunkel. He read while he masticated.

"Stagg," he said through a mouthful. "No question - I recognize the scrawl."

"Goddamn good thing the admiral didn't get that one," I said relieved. I was too close to retirement for a run in with that admiral - hell, any admiral. Kunkel chuckled a piece of sandwich out of his mouth. It stuck to the wind shield.

"What?" I inquired.

"Maybe he did," said Kunkel as he cleaned the lunch debris off the windshield.

"Bullshit Dave, we're not giving that note to the admiral." I said thinking of retirement again.

"No, no, Smitty. We just tell Stagg the admiral got it."

We laughed like hell. The boredom was quickly replaced by the enthusiasm of hatching a plot. I stashed the note in my pocket. When the admiral returned we took off and I'll be damned if he didn't ask for that box lunch before we cleared the stadium walls. That was close.

We got back to the air station just before the change of duty sections. Stagg was still in the OPS center when Dave Kunkel and I walked in. A giant grin smeared his face. He thought, he had messed with us.

"Did you get my love note, sir?" asked Stagg.

The moment was so delicious that I almost gave it all away, unable to control my Pavlovian drool.

"Stagg, you moron. The admiral got the lunch with the note in it." I said.

Stagg went into traumatic arrest. He stood stiff at attention and shook uncontrollably. He was ashen faced. While Kunkel read him the riot act, I used the phone in another office to call Kunkel in the OPS office. Kunkel distracted Stagg with an unabated castigation of his mental fitness. Stagg blubbered in response. Kunkel answered my call ringing on the OPS desk without missing a beat.

"Tell him it's the District Headquarters Chief of Staff and the admiral wants to see him at 10 AM. tomorrow morning" I told Kunkel.

"Yes sir," Kunkel replied.

I stepped back into the OPS office just as Kunkel was telling Stagg the admiral wanted to see him.

"Oh! No!" Stagg gasped. "How did he know it was me, sir?" he whined.

"I had to tell him Terry. He had that note in my face while chewing on my ear the whole way back. He knew we would recognize the writing. He's not stupid you know - that's why he's the admiral and you're not," I replied.

The hand wringing and head shaking continued as he left for home. His head hung down to his belt and he mumbled about the end of his career as he left the OPS Center. We could see him in his car out in the parking lot, gesticulating and shaking his head as he drove off.

The next day he showed up in dress blues. Earlier I had let my friend Jim Wright at the District Intel Office in on the gag. He agreed to call, playing the role as the District Chief of Staff, confirming Stagg's appointment with the admiral. Wright called about ten minutes after Stagg arrived. Stagg took the call at attention. By now everybody in the OPS Center was in on the gag and it was all we could do to keep still.

He was ashen faced again. His career was over because of a stupid prank. Guys were playing pranks on him all the time and their careers weren't over - he continued his stunned drone out of the OPS Center.

We let him get to his car before we called him back over the PA system. We told him the truth and he damn neared cried from the relief. Stagg took two or three days off to recuperate and when he returned to work, he spoke to no one in the officer corps for weeks - except to say, "sir."

HEY MAN

Towards the end of my career in New Orleans I was on a SAR flight looking for some fishing vessel out of Grand Isle, Louisiana. When you're stationed in New Orleans the SAR flights are always for, "out of Grand Isle." Because of that fact, the Union Oil dock in Grand Isle had initiated a policy of refueling Coast Guard helicopters for free. They even provided box lunches for the crew when we landed there. They knew most of the SAR flights were for their people. It promoted one hell of a lot of good will.

I had just landed an H-3 from a six-hour search for such a vessel - out of Grand Isle. While I was getting the box lunches back to the crew, I heard a very familiar voice over the din of the dockside chatter.

"Hey man, what for you did 'dat?" It said.

It was Chico. Even mixed with the cacophony of dockside noises and voices, I could recognize that sing song coonass cadence of his, after sixteen years since last hearing it.

I turned to search out the source and there on the dock was a little fat guy. His back was to me.

"Hey Chico," I yelled.

He was walking away and did not respond immediately. I yelled again.

"Hey Chico, it's me man."

He turned and said, "Yeah what I can do for ya?"

Then he recognized me and ran, launching his considerable girth and all 200 plus pounds into my arms. "Smitty, my man." he said as he jumped wrapping his legs around me.

Chico was the manager of the Union Oil dock at Grand Isle. He and his Coast Guard background were largely responsible for the refueling deal. The box lunches from Chico were exceptional.

THE LAST ONE

I was called out from New Orleans on a baleful night of 30 knot winds and 20 foot seas. The call was to one of the East Cameron Blocks in the Gulf of Mexico, which are rife with oil production platforms and drilling rigs. The Captain of a fishing boat had a excruciating case of kidney stones. I was with one of my dearest friends, an aviator who went on to become a true Coast Guard hero. His name is John Whiddon. John was a young Englishmen who immigrated to America as a child. He had declined acceptance into the British Royal Navy for pilot training to join the Coast Guard. He was a lieutenant junior grade that night and my co-pilot.

We crabbed and tacked our way the entire 120 miles to the East Cameron Blocks of the Gulf. Our bodies jarred in rhythmic sinc to the gusting wind that relentlessly buffeted the Sikorsky H-3 helicopter. We found the boat easily enough despite it's mere sixty feet. It bobbed like the cork it was, in the heavy seas despite it's extended trawling booms. The helmsman had all he could manage to hold her into them. Seas of this magnitude require some height between the vessel and the aircraft due to the enormous rise and fall of her deck. Consequently the helicopter must be well above the crest of the wave and off to one side, preferably the pilot's. You just can't hover over the deck, drop the basket and be on your merry way, not in seas and winds like these. And you can't just lower the basket on the winch either. In these conditions if the basket were not tethered by a tugger line on the deck, it would hook some rigging and drag the aircraft down into the trough where the rotors could stir the foam.

Our skilled air crew at the hoist and door, expertly threw the monkey fisted end of a tugger line down to the deck and secured the other to our rescue basket. On the hoist operators signal I waited. The boats top whip antenna kept appearing in my field of vision and fell away from view, only to reappear as the boat crested another enormous swell. That scared the lunch out of my bucket. If that antenna had so much as nicked the rotor, it would have all been over right there.

It always amazed me how under these conditions our aircrews performed so well. These guys were as precisely skilled and dedicated as any pilot. They gave the instructions that made the rescue work - two feet to the right - six feet up. Try finding those coordinates in the pitch of night with the wind trying to blow you into the sea. But we did what they said and the whole thing worked. People got rescued.

I held the aircraft as steady as possible while, Whiddon ticked off the instrument readings, as I was otherwise optically distracted from the gauges while craning to glean even a peripheral view of the scene below. The hoist man slowly payed out cable as the deck crew stripped in the tugger to keep the basket under a tight line. Slowly it made an angular descent. The hoist man yelled instructions into the hot mic over the din of engines, rotor and wind. As the boat deck rose and fell in the sea he called out, up, down, left and right. I followed his instructions thus using the helicopter to compensate for the slack or tension in the cable and line caused by the roll of the sea. The hoist man payed out cable in the same effort. As he did, the boat lurched and the cable slacked catching his lip mic and ripping it out of his helmet - one second I was receiving hover adjustment instructions and the next all I could hear was the wind howling in the hot mic, then nothing.

This was a serious problem. Even with the flood and hover lights on neither John nor I could see the deck. We didn't know what the boat was doing down there. As quick as all this transpired the radioman jumped from his seat to take over the call from the hoist man. It was the most beautiful example of teamwork I have ever seen. Not a beat was missed. I asked what happened and was told..

Finally the basket was on the deck with the ship's Captain inside. Now we had to pick it all up off a six by eight foot area of deck festooned with rigging and antennas. The procedure required I move the aircraft back in directly over the load and lift up through the obstacles, then move off to the side while the hoist man retrieved the load - our victim/patient, the captain.

From eighty or so feet above the deck, I was just about to do this when the boat dropped off the crest into the trough of a wave. The basket and captain were in midair one second and the next crashing side long into the next wave.

The aircrew yelled, "Man in the water!" I thought the captain had fallen out of basket and into the sea. But then the aircrew yelled again,

"Man and basket out of the water, take it up - up -up !"

I pulled up the collective hard and high. John called out our altitude -
"100 - 200 -300- 400 feet, Mal."

It was then that I heard a noise like a gigantic zipper being unzipped. It
came from underneath the aircraft. I turned to ask John what the hell that
was but he was looking out his window.

"Bloody hell, Mal! - Look at this," he said.

I looked across the cockpit past his profiled and gaping jaw to see the
captain and the basket tethered to the end of the hoist cable. A look of sheer
terror covered his face. I will never forget the size of the mans open eyes. Like
saucers they were - nor his white knuckles glowing in the reflected light of the
flood and hovers. It was a death grip. That quick he was gone from view.
John and I turned our heads in unison to look out my window and a second
later he appeared on that side of the aircraft. Still terrified and still clutching
the sides of the rescue basket in fists of steel held closed by hydraulic tendons.
He was victim to a great 80 foot deranged pendulum who's arc decreased with
each turn of the hoist drum, thus increasing the speed a frequency of the
swing. The zipper noise was the hoist cable grating across the bottom of the
aircraft as it was being wound while the basket was at the end of it's arc.

All I could do was hold the aircraft still while the hoist man reeled him
in. As the cable shortened the load swung faster in shorter arcs until it bashed
against the under side of the helicopter. And then the radioman said he was
level with the door and the crew managed to get the load inside.

With the guy inside the aircraft I asked John to take the controls. I
needed a minute to collect myself. I took many deep breathes. Once com-
posed I asked the crewman how our passenger (and victim) was doing.

"He has a compound fracture on his left fore arm from hitting the aircraft belly sir," said the radioman. "Oh yeah, he won't get out of the basket -
he's still got a grip on the basket rail. I can't pry his hands loose."

"Leave him there," I said.

We flew fast to the nearest hospital in New Orleans. As we approached
I had the radioman call in to advise them of an arriving emergency with kidney stones and a compound fracture of the left arm. They wanted to know
who he was and if he had insurance. Then they didn't want to take him when

I couldn't provide the information. I finally convinced them that I was setting down in their parking lot and they better have a gurney ready or they would be responsible for leaving a busted up guy unattended.

A doctor, nurse and orderly cowered in our rotor wash behind a gurney as I set down in their parking lot. They took him. I never heard any more about the incident. It was my last SAR flight.

WRECK OF THE 1423

Early one morning during my 2nd tour in Kodiak I was called to respond to the scene of a capsized tugboat in the Cook Inlet. The waters of the Cook Inlet are notoriously treacherous. Every year dozens of boats and lives are lost to its' hidden rocks and widely fluctuating tides. It was in the Cook Inlet that the intrepid Captain James Cook lost his anchor to the outgoing tide at what is now called Anchor Point, just some twenty miles northwest of our destination - Homer on the lower end of the Kenai Peninsula.

Perfunctory and preflight completed, LCDR Lee Goforth and myself launched for the two hour flight to Homer. I was the AC. The weather was miserable and we had to fly our single engine Sikorsky H-52 at about one hundred feet off the deck because that was the extent of our ceiling. Under that ceiling we had only about a half mile of visibility A C-130 out of Kodiak was also dispatched to accompany our flight at twenty thousand feet, for two reasons. The first and foremost, since the H-52 had no radar, was to be our eyes with their radar - a "seeing eye plane", for a couple of handicapped pilots. They guided us on a northeast vector from Kodiak to Homer around the Afognak Island area and Tonki Cape, which boasts mountains in the two thousand foot range, then past the Barren Islands. At one hundred feet, we couldn't see shit, let alone any geographical features. The deplorable conditions were only worsened by the salt spray and wind driven rain hitting the windshield. It was a nerve wracking, white knuckle flight and the leg to Homer would only be the first part of it. Hell, we still had to land in Homer, refuel from the C-130 (the 2nd reason it had accompanied us) and then go find the capsized tug. So the able and skilled crew of the C-130 guided us with their radar through the treacherous peaks on Afongnak, Shuyak and the Barren Islands.

The radio chatter between us and the 130 was somewhat light and humorous with a nervous twist. I chided the C-130 crew that if they flew me into the side of a mountain - they should pray that I died in the crash - because I would hunt them down for a merciless payback.

"I know where you guys work," I said. The co-pilot of the C-130, Gerry Zanoli, chuckled and assured us not to worry.

When we had the Homer Spit in sight, the C-130 landed and we followed in over the Spit to land and refuel from it, at the Homer Airport. I asked Lee to take the controls so I could close out the flight plan for the tug with the Anchorage center. He did so and landed the chopper on the tarmac behind the C-130 which had proceeded us by a few minutes.

Lee set the chopper down at the five o'clock position behind the big aircraft which put us just aft and starboard of the big lumbering beast's tail. We shut down and the 130's crew prepared to refuel us. It was a tight fit due to the snow banks that were plowed up and off the edges of the tarmac. Because Homer is also a commercial airport the tower had put the C-130 well off to one side so as not to interfere with commercial or private aviation, of which Homer has plenty.

The C-130 had about one hundred feet of fuel hose, that any ground refueling could be accomplished at an optimum distance. But we just couldn't get any further away. There was no room to extend further back and away from the C-130. Lee had set her down in exactly the right and only spot available. Lee and I hopped out to stay out of the way during refueling.

While we were in the Homer terminal building filing the flight plan for the tug search one of the crewmen from the C-130 came to advise me that they were ready to get airborne but the pilot thought our Sikorsky was a little too close and was very concerned about prop wash blowing the chopper over when he started his engines and applied taxi power to the throttle. It would take him a few minutes to reach altitude, so logically he had to launch first. - The 130 pilot was hesitant to do it with the #1423 sitting some forty feet away off his five o'clock position.

This seemed reasonable to me. We were a little close. I looked out the window of the terminal building window and thought, "that's a little tight, I can move off to the starboard a little more out of the 130's prop wash." "I can move it - there's room to maneuver," I assured myself.

"You want me to take that Mal?" Lee asked.

"Nah, I got it. Hey Lee, get us some coffee. We gotta' wait for him to get to altitude so we have a little time - be right back."

I yelled for our crewman to follow me and went to move the chopper so the 130 could get airborne and continue to guide us through our search pattern.

Even though the search would be conducted over open water we still needed that 130 overhead to keep us out of trouble while vectoring us to the scene.

I instructed the crewman to stand well out of the rotor wash and signal me with his arms to indicate the amount of space between the Sikorksy's main rotor and the tail section of the C-130. We planned our move and I jumped in the seat to fire up the chopper. Once the engine reached the optimum RPM, I signaled the crewman that I was ready to proceed and he signaled back to begin taxiing the aircraft.

I still don't know how it happened. Either I misread the signal or the crewman gave the wrong signal or both. It was only seconds into the maneuver when the choppers main rotor tore into the starboard aft stabilizer of the C-130.

All hell broke loose and I mean, LOOSE. The crewman set the land speed record for "get outta there". The chopper shook and bucked so much, it created a strobe effect as I watched everyone within sight "skee-daddle." Helpless in the cockpit all I could do was hang on to the cyclic stick while the Sikorsky's main rotor shredded about 2 feet off the 130's starboard tail stabilizer. If I let go the whole shooting match was going to start flopping like a fish on a stringer.

Instantly, the sound of metal rending drowned out even the engine noise of the chopper.

It is, a sound I will never forget. I just knew I was dead.

Within seconds of the initial contact with the C-130 everything stopped. Those few seconds of course seemed an eternity of slow motion, accentuated by the strobe effect of the bucking aircraft and wobbling rotor. Finally I came to my senses and looked down at my hands, still with a death grip on the stick. Both my thumbs were dislocated back up my wrists. The inside of my thighs felt like they had been pummeled with a ball peen hammer from the stick beating them. My chest and lap were covered in red liquid.

"Oh Christ! I am dead," I thought.

I reached for the battery switch to cut the power. That reaction was rote. I did not want any electrical current running around the circuitry while I was still in the cockpit, but hit the wipers instead. When they came on I knew I was still alive and had at least one arm still attached. I tried for the battery switch again but this time my hand passed through a pulsating stream of red liquid.

"My blood," I thought.

I put my hand to my chest in a feeble effort to stem the flow.

"How strange," I thought as the blood continued to squirt right through my palm. Then I realized it wasn't squirting out of me - it was squirting on me - it was a ruptured hydraulic line to the rotor brake.

With that realization, my senses became acute and I swatted the battery toggle into the off position with my almost useless hand. I had to get out of there. The smell of AV gas, smoke and hydraulic fluid told me it was time to go. The whine of the compass gyros coasting down gave the whole scene an eerie resonance.

"Never exit a downed helicopter while the rotor is still turning," I mumbled to myself. I looked up through the windshield for the rotor. It wasn't turning - hell, it wasn't even there.

I pushed myself up and out of the seat, which was no mean feat without any thumbs, turned to exit the aircraft between the seats and out the side cabin door. The radio rack had been ripped completely off its' mounts. It lay in a twisted jumble right behind the pilots seats. I had to jump over it. I caught my boot lace or flight suit on something sharp and landed on my knees next to the cabin door. Thank God it was open because I never would have managed with my thumbs dislocated.

Outside the cabin door on the tarmac lay the H-52's main rotor and transmission. I had to jump over the whole mess and landed on the tarmac, knees down again. I was covered in hydraulic fluid and God knows what other flammable liquids. I was a human wick just waiting for a match.

I got to my feet and ran for the nearest snow bank, like a dog with a Korean chef after him. I figured if I got in the snow I would not burn, no matter what else happened. I dove head first into the snow bank. I thought I was okay until I couldn't get a breath. I was suffocating.

"Oh great," I thought. Here, I'd survived the wreckage only to suffocate in a snowbank.

"Just great," I thought again.

I kicked and flailed my legs to no avail. I was just about to pass out when some crew from the C-130 pulled me out by the ankles.

Whenever a crash or accident occurs, a thorough investigation follows. And this was the case with the incident involving the H-52 #1423 and the C-130.

Several weeks later, after my thumbs had returned to normal function, I sat in an office at the Kodiak CGAS, behind the desk was Commander somebody - I can not remember the guy's name.

He started with a series of nonincident related questions such as my name rank, serial number, duty station etc. About an hour into the interview he noticed that his tape recorder was not running. I must have rattled him with my cool demeanor and he neglected to turn it on.

"We'll have to do this interview all over again LCDR Smith," he said.

"The hell you say, sir," said I. "You'll just have to write all that up from memory - maybe you should have taken notes, sir," I said emphatically.

"No, we'll have to do this over," said the commander.

"Sir, I have given you my statement and that really is all I have to say," I replied.

And with that I left the room. The interview was over. The commander however did not think so and marched his inquiring little butt down the hall to my CO's office, to complain that I was not cooperating with his investigation. I followed to defend myself and I knew the CO would want to see about this as well.

He made his case to Captain Hogue, my CO, who told the investigating officer, "Well, commander you had better remember what he said."

"May I ask the LCDR one more question?" the inquisitor requested of my CO.

"Answer the man's last question, Smitty."

"Yes sir," I agreed.

"Mr. Smith, *why* did you hit that C-130 with your aircraft?" he queried

I thought the top of my head would come off. I could feel my guts churning in anger and my eyes went to slits as I stared him down. *Why?* That was a completely ludicrous question. *Why*, implies that I had some ulterior motive to wreck an H-52 Sikorsky and severely damage a C-130. What the hell did this guy think - that I deliberately tried to abort the rescue mission by wrecking my chopper - or what? I fumed, my glower intensified. He should have asked [how] - NOT WHY!

"Well, Mr. Smith can you tell me why you hit the C-130 with your aircraft?" he asked again.

Now, all I could see was red. I really wanted to choke him. But, my years of training in dealing with idiotic situations prevented me from moving. I just took a deep breath .

"I'll tell you why commander - I never liked those C-130's anyway," I quipped.

Phil Houge chuckled through his ubiquitous cigar. "Dismissed gentlemen," he said and flicked his hand toward the door.

The interview was definitely over.

Several weeks after the interview I received a non judicial letter of admonishment from the Commander 17th Coast Guard District. A formal reproval if you will and like most military documents it contained far to many words. It went on and on with whereas I did this and that. And I should have done such and such instead of what I did. It continued with statements such as, "how a pilot of your experience and tenure could attempt such a maneuver..."

However, the part that struck me the funniest were these words... "Therefore you are administratively admonished to be more careful in the exercise of your judgment in the future." And with that, the #1423 incident was closed. So I thought.

Epilogue

In June of 1991, almost fourteen years after my retirement, I was living in St. Petersburg, Florida happily self-employed as the owner/broker of a real estate office. The Coast Guard Air Station at St. Pete had been relocated to Clearwater about twenty miles to the north of it's former location at Albert Whitted Field. Retirement did not keep me from enjoying all my wonderful friends from the Coast Guard and I still had some old buddies stationed at Clearwater. The commanding officer there, Captain Jerry Heinz and I had been friends for many years and we stayed in regular contact through monthly luncheons and visits. Clearwater was rife with my old compadres. They were in every department of the Air Station - CDR Dave Kunkel, was the engineering officer, CDR Darrell Nelson (Ed Nelson's eldest son) and CDR Terry Stagg were in operations and many others too numerous to mention served by their sides. I was proud every time I saw those guys.

With these connections to my past so close at hand I was not surprised to receive a call from Dave Kunkel one afternoon. After all the years and the incident with the Stagg lunches, considering his capacity to plot, and willing propensity to lie, I should have been leery of Dave Kunkel. But I was retired and relished any opportunity to associate with my old comrades. My guard was down. Dave invited me to a retirement "do" over in Mobile. He said a C-130 was going over with a group of other retired Coasties from Clearwater for "some guys retirement", and a tour of all the new simulator equipment a the training center. The CO, Jerry Heinz would fly with Terry Stagg as Co-Pilot. Did I want to go?

Well you can imagine my answer. This was a chance for a nice little flight over to Mobile with a bunch of my old buddies, and I could see some others in Mobile. Hell yeah! I wanted to go. I arrived early the next morning to an OPS Center full of retired Coasties. Soon Jerry and Terry arrived with Kunkel in tow. We loaded and launched for Mobile. It was just like the good old days. Man, I felt good to be with these guys again, in the air - it couldn't get any better than this.

Once we reached cruising altitude I walked around the cabin and shot the breeze with the likes of Ken Gard, Bob Whitley, Dan Shorey and others. I asked just about everybody, as I moved along the length of the plane, who was retiring. No one knew. Lemmings to the sea I thought. The mention of a free ride and lunch could draw them out of the woodwork. But then, I was with them.

Two hours later we touched down at Bates Field in Mobile and taxied over to the Coast Guard Air Station ramp. We were met and greeted individually by the Air Station and Training Center Commander, Captain Paul Busick. He shook our hands and welcomed us profusely. As the group chatted, there on the tarmac, Paul sidled up to me. He insisted that I try my hand at the new simulators and make a few runs on them. I thought the special attention by Paul a bit odd considering the magnitude of the other guy's rank and accomplishment. Alright, I can be gracious. I could use a little stroking in my old age.

We spent all afternoon running simulators for the new Falcon and H-60 aircraft.

I was impressed and a little jealous of the young kids that were flying with these new tools. At the end of the day we toured the base, then Paul invited me for coffee at his office and we caught up since last I saw him in New Orleans. After coffee he suggested we take a walk back over to the simulator building because there was one other piece of equipment he thought I would enjoy. Then to the O' Club for drinks, where the retirement was to take place. I agreed of course.

At the training center he pointed to a specific door. I opened it see one hundred guys standing around the room. I excused myself for interrupting and began to back out but in unison they cajoled me further in. All the guys from the C-130 ride were mixed among the throng. Wearily, I stepped back into the room, greeted by cheers and smiles. I got the distinct feeling something was up. I was the only lemming on that flight.

Paul quieted the group and directed my attention to a large object on the far side of the room. It was draped in a sheet and tied with a large red ribbon and bow. Something was definitely up. He walked across the room in silence and under the light of smiling faces, aglow with the look I had come to recognize all too often during my career. Something was up. At the draped object, he turned and pulled the ribbon, dropping the sheet to the floor.

There, again, before my eyes was my old friend and protector, my shield from death, the cockpit of H-52, #1423. A handsome brass plaque attached to the side certified it's origin and donor - Homer and me. She had been salvaged after her encounter with the 130 and turned to the only duty her truncated form could serve, a cockpit training implement. Poor old girl, for nineteen long years she had served faithfully. With the retirement of the H-52 from the Coast Guard's inventory, her usefulness was outlived. I knew the feeling.

As I stood before her, a tear welled in the corner of my eye while Paul presented me with her tail rotor blade. Its plaque was inscribed with further certification of the only other salvageable piece of that aircraft's unauthorized modification on April 19, 1972. It hangs in my den now.

Before adjourning to the O Club for drinks and further cheer, Captain Busick read and presented me with a Certificate of Merit attesting to my futuristic vision and heroism regarding the incident. Now I had both a letter of admonition and a Certificate of Merit for the Wreck of the #1423. How the pendulum 'do swing.

"Who the hell is retiring?" I bellowed. They all ignored me. Something else was up.

"Let's go," said Paul and we made our way to the club.

At the O Club, I was further surprised to find there wasn't a retirement at all. It was a roast scheduled in my honor. Then I was delighted to find my old friend Captain George Krietemeyer, USCG, (retired) as MC. George and Paul took turns for the rest of the evening, telling story after story in which I starred. I didn't learn until later that George and Paul had made arrangements for the #1423 cockpit trainer to be put on permanent display at the Naval Aviation Museum in Pensacola. She sits there today in well deserved rest - kind of like the rest of us. I can never express my thanks to those guys for the most wonderful evening of my career in Mobile, Alabama on that January night in 1991 - fourteen years after the fact and almost twenty after the incident. When I think or speak the names, Dave Kunkel, Paul Busick, George Krietemeyer, Jerry Heinz and all the others, the memories flood back to me in great flashes. Thanks you guys.

And so it is, that I have only this to tell, though out of sequence in the grand passage of time this text relates, it is noteworthy and appropriate to bear mention at it's conclusion.

In January of 1969 the Coast Guard was retiring the Sikorsky H-52 for the H-3 Pelican. This meant that every rotary wing pilot had to train and qualify on the H-3. This training cycle left a void of available pilots in New Orleans and I was assigned TAD (temporary additional duty) to augment those crews. I am not sure whether my skill as a SAR pilot or luck of the draw got me the assignment, but I went down from E-City for a few weeks to relieve the duty section pilots while they trained.

One dark and stormy night I had the duty and I was accompanied by Lieutenant Junior Grade Terry Beacham who was the brother of one of my oldest and dearest friends, Connelly Beacham. Terry displayed every bit the colorful character of his brother, but it was cloaked in the dignity an officer is supposed to carry. We were out among the oil field platforms in weather that slapped the stuffing out of us. I was having a tough time of it and I know he was. Hell, I had done this kind of thing for years and it was getting to me. Terry was only a junior grade with neither callous nor hair upon his ass. I know he was shook up.

He turned to me at the worst of it and said, "Sheee-it! Mal this is bad. Let's do a 360 and get out of here!"

I looked at him with a smile, banked the helo into a turn and did just that. I think now would be the perfect time, to take Terry's advise again.

WHERE ARE THEY NOW?

Rear Adm. Dave Kunkel - Still active, Head Interagency Task Force, another good guy made good.

Cmdr. Terry Stagg - Seminole, Florida, still the perfect ensign and friend.

Cmdr. John Whiddon - Kodiak, Alaska , Owns a seafood cannery, a pure superstar.

Vice Adm. Deese Thompson - North Carolina, It just doesn't get any better than this.

Connelly Beachum - Somewhere over Albemarle Sound, smiling.

Lt. Cmdr. Harold "Charlie" Brown - Unknown but probably playing the guitar.

Capt. Tom Carter - Houston, Texas, Still smiling, what a great teacher.

Adm. Owen Siler - My first Coast Guard idol, still owe him the cleaning bill.

Capt. George Krietemeyer - Mobile, Alabama. All the Pterodactyls owe him.

Cmdr. J.V.A. Thompson - Deceased, probably buying and selling in the great beyond.

Vice Adm. Dick Herr - Maryland, Best example that all nice guys don't finish last.

ADCM Victor Bearinger - Mobile, Retired and enjoying his 5 daughters.

Rear Adm. Ed Nelson - Astoria, Oregon., My mentor, still.

Capt. Darrell Nelson - Still active and back at HQ, a chip off the ole' block.

Tom Binford - Florida, Taking on the legal profession, the best ex-brother-in-law. Author of *Legal Whores*.

Cmdr. Al Pell - Making a deal somewhere.

Lt. Cmdr. Billy Ed Murphy - Bicoastal, California and Florida, could have joined the pro tour.

BMC Marcus Patterson - Hopefully working for someone like himself.

Seaman Tom Brothers - Most likely the CEO of a Fortune 500 company.

AL3 Perry " Chico" Chighizola - The purest coon ass, last known Grand Isle, Louisiana.

Dr. Hans Windenburg - Most likely a brain surgeon in Austin, Texas.

Cmdr. James "Frannie" Wright - Parker, Colorado, retired from United Airlines, practicing his darts and golf.

Capt. Jerry Zanoli - Living in L.A. thinking about joining the senior tour.

Capt. Marty Kaiser - Practicing law in St. Petersburg, Florida, and enjoying life.

Lt. Cmdr. Dave Simpson, Running hardware store in the Cayman Islands, just lucky to be alive.

Larry Williams - Living in California, still wondering why he didn't stay in the Coast Guard with me.

Capt. Phil Hogue - Deceased and fondly remembered.

Cmdr. Preston McMillan - Unknown, but possibly polishing his Bentley.

Cmdr. Harry Hutchens - Living in the North West, missing J-Vat's company.

Rear Adm. Paul Busick - High level security, practicing his fly fishing.

Capt. Jerry Heinz - Deceased, without a doubt residing in heaven.

Capt.Fred Merritt - Deceased, hopefully flying around in a UFO.

Capt. Basil Harrington - Making all the souls above smile. Basil was a very smart man.

Capt. Dave Bosomworth - E-City, real estate tycoon, gotta' be raising coon dogs.

ATCS Bill Hecker - Truly retired somewhere in the South.

BMC Darwin Rennewanz - Kodiak, Alaska, retired my old Captain of the Port, buddy.

Cmdr. Bruce Melnick - Florida, you made us all proud.

Cmdr. Jim Webb - Deceased but never forgotten, "Webb!"

Cmdr. Paul Smith - Bourg, Louisiana., my hand still hurts from catching his pitches.

ALCS John Timmons - Unfortunately unknown.

Lt. Chris Nelson - St. Petersburg, Florida, World renowned dermatologist.

Cmdr. Jim Boteler - North Carolina, still flying for American Airlines.

Cmdr. Chuck Peterson - Wisconsin, Still making folks smile.

Cmdr. Bill Ricks - E- City, Looks a lot older than his age, served as county tax collector, always well liked in the Coast Guard.

MALCOLM R. SMITH

Malcolm R. Smith was born in San Diego, California in 1940. He joined the Coast Guard in 1957 on a dare under the " buddy system" with his lifelong friend Larry Williams. "It was the best mistake I ever made," he said. During his career with the Coast Gaurd he was awarded; Air Medal, (2), Coast Guard Commendation Medal, (2 w/"O"), Coast Guard Unit Commendation (2), Coast Guard Meritorious Unit Commendation Ribbon, (2), Coast Guard Good Conduct Medal (2), and the National Defense Service Medal.

After retirement in October 1977, he has owned an art gallery and a commercial real estate firm. He currently lives outside of Aspen, Colorado with his wife Diane where he enjoys all outdoor activities. He is the proud father of four daughters: Kelly, Holly, Wendy, Angela, and two grandchildren.

J. WILFRED CAHILL

J. Wilfred Cahill was born in Winooski, Vermont in 1949 and raised in Hicksville and Buffalo, New York, Salt Lake City and St. Paul. He graduated high school in Bel Air, Maryland then attended the College of St. Scholastica. Since 1985 he and his bride of 27 years, Bonita, have owned and operated a successful real estate and property management firm in Aspen, Colorado. He is the proud father of an only daughter, Ashe. Since meeting Malcolm Smith in 1992, Cahill has become the de facto Colorado Fly Fishing Guide for the Coast Guard retirees. He splits his time in Colorado between Carbondale, operating his business and Olathe, writing, woodworking and fishing.

PRISCILLA MESSNER-PATTERSON

Priscilla Messner-Patterson and her husband Butch, a pilot for the U.S. Fish & Wildlife Service, have lived on Kodiak Island in the Gulf of Alaska since 1983. Although she occasionally paints other subjects, her primary focus is aviation related, often featuring general aviation, historical Alaskan themes and the U.S. Coast Guard. She has been a member of the American Society of Aviation Artists since 1994. She is also a member of the Canadian Aviation Artists Association, the Alaskan Watercolor Society and both the Coast Guard and Air Force programs. Priscilla was the recipient of the ASAA Gold Founders' Award at the 2002 Forum in Savannah and an Award of Merit from the Simuflite 2002 Exhibition in Dallas. For information on limited editions, original paintings or commissions, please contact the artist at P.O. Box 3348, Kodiak, Alaska 99615.

Phone 907 486 8447 - Web site - www.bearlymattersstudio.com

ISBN 141200407-1